# KING

## Don't Beg, They Make Decrees

### Claiming Your Royal Identity & Declaring Your Destiny

By

## Nick Imoru

**Achievers Publishing**
Calgary, Canada

# KINGS DO NOT BEG, THEY MAKE DECREES



ISBN: 978-1-989291-08-5

Published in Canada, by
**Achievers Publishing**

**Canadian Cataloguing in Publication (CIP)**
A Record of this Publication is available from the Library and Archives Canada (LAC).



For further information or permission, address:
**Achievers Publishing**
Calgary, Canada
E-mail: info@achieverspublishing.com
www.achieverspublishing.com

Printed in Canada for Achievers Publishing

# KING

## Don't Beg,
## They Make Decrees

Claiming Your Royal Identity
& Declaring Your Destiny

# DEDICATION

This book is dedicated to all believers, chosen by God to walk in the reality of kingship and priesthood—a divine appointment not of our own making, nor one we ever asked for, but a gift from our loving Father.

To the sons and daughters of the King, may you embrace the truth that:

*"Kings don't beg, they decree. They have only one destiny, and that's to reign. God has made you king. Reign and rule, refuse to beg!"* — *Chris Oyakhilome*

May this book inspire you to step boldly into your destiny, exercising the authority, power, and purpose God has bestowed upon you. Reign as the king He has called you to be!

# TABLE OF CONTENTS

Contents

~ 16 ~

# INTRODUCTION

## Why I wrote this Book?

On the early morning of Tuesday, April 24, 2018, during a seemingly ordinary moment while taking a shower, I was suddenly and profoundly inspired to write a book titled "Kings Don't Beg, They Make Decrees." This moment of divine inspiration was more than a passing thought; it was a clear and direct message from God. As I continued with my day, particularly during my train ride to work, God began to reveal to me the depth and the content of what needed to be written. The message was unmistakable, and the scriptures began to come alive with new meaning, providing a blueprint for the book you now hold in your hands.

## Chosen and Empowered: A Call to Kingship

The foundation of this book lies in the truth that as believers, we are called to a royal and priestly identity. This concept is rooted in scriptures like Exodus 19:5, where God declares, *"Now therefore, if you will in fact obey My voice and keep My covenant (agreement), then you shall be My own special possession and treasure from among all peoples [of the world], for all the earth is Mine"* (AMP). This passage speaks to the unique and elevated position we hold as God's chosen people—a theme that resonates throughout this book.

We see this royal identity further emphasized in 1 Peter 2:9-10, which proclaims, *"But ye are a chosen generation, a royal priesthood, an holy nation, a peculiar people; that ye should shew forth the praises of him who hath called you out of darkness into his marvellous light"* (KJV). This verse highlights the dual role we possess as both kings and priests, called not only to rule but also to intercede, to stand in the gap for others before God.

## Understanding the Dual Role: King and Priest

It is crucial to understand that in Christ, we are not merely kings or priests; we are both. This dual role is vital because, as a king, we are endowed with authority, but as a priest, we have access to the throne of grace. Our kingship gives us the authority to decree, to speak things into existence according to the will of God. Psalm 110:4 affirms our priestly role, stating, *"The LORD hath sworn, and will not repent, Thou art a priest for ever after the order of Melchizedek"* (KJV).

As kings, we have the authority given to us as children of the Most High God. Romans 8:17 tells us, *"And if children, then heirs; heirs of God, and joint-heirs with Christ."* This means we share in Christ's authority, empowering us to do the works that He did and even greater works, as Jesus Himself promised in John 14:12-14. We are commissioned to bring others into the Kingdom of God, as highlighted in the Great Commission (Matthew 28:18-20).

However, our priestly role is just as critical. As priests, we have direct access to God's throne of grace. Hebrews 4:16 encourages us, *"Let us therefore come boldly to the throne of grace, that we may obtain mercy and find grace to help in time of need*" (NKJV). This access allows us to intercede on behalf of others, standing in the gap just as Christ, our ultimate High Priest, continually intercedes for us (Hebrews 7:24-25).

## The Importance of Recognizing Our Identity

This book was written to awaken believers to their true identity and to encourage them to walk in the authority and access they have been given. Deuteronomy 7:6 (KJV) underscores our unique status, *"For thou art an holy people unto the LORD thy God: the LORD thy God hath chosen thee to be a special people unto himself, above all people that are upon the face of the earth."* As God's special possession, we are not called to live in defeat or lack; we are called to reign in life, to make decrees, and to see them established.

Isaiah 61:6 (NLT) declares, *"You will be called priests of the LORD, ministers of our God. You will feed on the treasures of the nations and boast in their riches."* This verse is a powerful reminder that our royal priesthood comes with both spiritual authority and tangible blessings. We are called to influence the world around us, to draw from the wealth of nations, and to manifest God's Kingdom here on earth.

In essence, this book is a guide for believers to step into their God-given roles as kings and priests. It is a call to understand the authority we carry, the access we have, and the responsibility that comes with being both a king and a priest. This revelation is not just for knowledge but for action—to empower you to live out your calling, to make decrees, and to see the Kingdom of God advance in every area of your life.

This book is not just about theory; it's about practical, biblical principles that you can apply to walk in the fullness of your identity in Christ. As you read through its pages, may you be inspired to take up your rightful place as a king and a priest, knowing that you have been chosen, empowered, and equipped to make a difference in this world for the glory of God.

## Purpose of the Book

The book *"Kings Do Not Beg, They Make Decrees"* is written to awaken believers to the reality of their identity and authority in Christ. The purpose of this book is to shift the mindset of Christians from one of dependency and helplessness to one of dominion and authority. As children of God, we are not called to live as beggars or victims of circumstances; rather, we are called to reign as kings, exercising the authority that has been bestowed upon us through Jesus Christ.

This book aims to dismantle the misconceptions that have kept many believers in a state of spiritual poverty and to replace them with the truth of who we are in Christ. Through a deep exploration of the scriptures and practical teachings, the book will guide you on how to walk in your God-given authority, make decrees, and see them established in your life.

The message of this book is not only just for the spiritually mature but it is for every believer who desires to live in the fullness of the life that God has provided. Whether you are new to the faith or have been walking with God for years, this book will challenge you to rise to the level of authority that God has intended for you. It will inspire you to speak boldly, act confidently, and live victoriously as a king in the Kingdom of God.

## Understanding the Authority of Kingship in Christ

At the heart of this book is the understanding that in Christ, we have been made kings and priests unto God. This royal identity is not just a title; it is a position of authority and responsibility that we are called to embrace and walk in. The Bible, in Revelation 1:6, says, *"And hath made us kings and priests unto God and his Father; to him be glory and dominion for ever and ever. Amen."* This verse reveals the dual roles we play in God's Kingdom—kings who reign and priests who intercede.

The authority of kingship in Christ is rooted in the finished work of Jesus on the cross. When Jesus declared, *"It is finished,"* He not only secured our salvation but also restored to us the authority that Adam lost in the Garden of Eden. This authority is not limited to a select few; it is available to every believer who is in Christ. As kings, we are called to make decrees that align with God's Word and to see those decrees established in our lives and the world around us.

Kingship in Christ means that we no longer approach God from a place of lack or desperation. Instead, we approach Him with confidence, knowing that He has already provided everything we need for life and godliness (2 Peter 1:3). Our prayers are not to be filled with begging and pleading, but with declarations of faith, thanksgiving, and authority. We are to speak to circumstances, command them to align with God's will, and expect to see results because our words carry the power of the King of kings.

Moreover, understanding our kingship in Christ also means recognizing that we are seated with Him in heavenly places, far above all principalities and powers (Ephesians 2:6). This spiritual position gives us the vantage point to rule and reign over all the works of the enemy. We are not subject to the ebbs and flows of life; rather, we are called to dominate them through the authority we have in Christ.

In this book, you will learn how to exercise this authority effectively. You will discover the power of making decrees and declarations, the importance of understanding your royal identity, and how to walk in the fullness of your kingship every day. The chapters that follow will equip you with the knowledge and tools you need to live as the king that God has made you to be.

As you journey through this book, let the truths within it sink deeply into your heart. Allow the Holy Spirit to open your eyes to the reality of your authority in Christ. And as you embrace your identity as a king, may you begin to experience the victory, prosperity, and dominion that come with living in the fullness of your kingship.

# CHAPTER 1

# BORN A SINNER, MADE A KING

Many Christians are familiar with this verse from the scriptures in 1 Peter 2:9:

*"But you are a chosen generation, a royal priesthood, a holy nation, His own special people, that you may proclaim the praises of Him who called you out of darkness into His marvelous light." —New King James Version (NKJV)*

While many believers recognize that this scripture speaks about the priesthood of believers, some are uncomfortable with the term "priesthood." There are mixed feelings among Christians about this verse. However, the Bible teaches not only the priesthood of the believer but also the royalty of the believer. This is where many Christians are almost completely unaware of the fact that we are also kings.

Understanding our identity in Christ—knowing who we are as believers—is the most important part of being a Christian. Being a Christian is not about keeping rules and regulations, performing rituals, or even attending church; it is about a friendship with Jesus Christ, which opens the door to a special relationship with God.

Historically, the first Gentile church was founded in Antioch, as recorded in Acts 11:19-26. The Christian community in Antioch began when Christians who were scattered from Jerusalem due to persecution fled to Antioch, where they were joined by Christians from Cyprus and Cyrene. It was in Antioch that the followers of Jesus were first called Christians:

*"And when he had found him, he brought him to Antioch. So it was that for a whole year they assembled with the church and taught a great many people. And the disciples were first called Christians in Antioch." — Acts 11:26 (NKJV)*

Therefore, a Christian is not merely someone who "treats other people in a kind or generous way" or "a member of a Christian denomination," as defined by some dictionaries. Rather, a Christian is a follower of Christ and has a special relationship with the Father.

Understanding our identity in Christ is essential if we are to enjoy the benefits of being true followers of Christ. While many Christians recognize that we are "priests," they often overlook that we are also "kings." Looking again at 1 Peter 2:9:

*"But you are a chosen generation, a royal priesthood, a holy nation, His own special people, that you may proclaim the praises of Him who called you out of darkness into His marvelous light." —New King James Version (NKJV)*

The rendering of this scripture emphasizes that we are recognized as "royal" before we are recognized as "priests." It says "a royal priesthood"—not just a priest, but a royal priest, thereby connecting us to kingship. This is further affirmed in Revelation 1:5-6:

*"and from Jesus Christ, the faithful witness, the firstborn from the dead, and the ruler over the kings of the earth.*

Here, we are directly referred to as "kings" and "priests." There is no ambiguity—we are kings. 1 Peter 2:9 calls us a royal priesthood, and Revelation 1:6 states that Christ has "made us kings and priests unto God." Unfortunately, many Christians feel uncomfortable when told they are priests, and they are often unaware that they are also kings.

## How Did We Become Kings?

The Bible says that Jesus Christ made us kings: *"and has made us kings and priests to His God and Father."* He made us kings when "He washed us from our sins in His own blood." He did this because "He loved us," and this love led Him to die on the Cross for us. We didn't ask Him to make us kings; it was not our intention or choice. It was His intention, His choice, and His idea. Why? Because He is a King Himself. As the Bible says:

*"For the Lord Most High is awesome; He is a great King over all the earth." —Psalm 47:2 (NKJV)*

He is the great King over all the earth, which is why He made us kings. In fact, He is the ruler over the kings of the earth:

*"and from Jesus Christ, the faithful witness, the firstborn from the dead, and the ruler over the kings of the earth."*

So, Jesus Christ is our King, making Him the King of all kings—the Ruler of all the kings over all the earth. Remember, when God created man, He gave him dominion over the whole earth. The Bible says in Genesis 1:26:

*"And God said, Let us make man in our image, after our likeness: and let them have dominion over the fish of the sea, and over the fowl of the air, and over the cattle, and over all the earth, and over every creeping thing that creepeth upon the earth." —King James Version (KJV)*

This scripture clearly confirms that God gave man dominion over everything on the earth. Dominion means "rule or power to rule; sovereign authority or control." Therefore, to have dominion means to rule or have the power to rule over all the earth. However, it's important to understand that the dominion God gave to man was over everything except other people. Dominion over mankind belongs to God alone.

God has placed you on earth to govern it and reign as a king, meaning you are to excel in your area of specialty, pursuit, study, or skill in which you have devoted much time and effort and in which you are an expert.

What does this mean? It means that man is totally responsible for whatever happens on earth. You are responsible for the outcome of your life and what happens on the earth. Therefore, man can only permit God to influence his activities on earth through prayer by asking God. However, man forfeited this privilege after his fall.


## The Fall of Man

After God created the first man, Adam, He planted a beautiful garden called Eden and placed Adam there:

*"Now the Lord God had planted a garden in the east, in Eden; and there he put the man he had formed." — Genesis 2:8 (New International Version, NIV)*

Adam was to live in this garden, raising the question of what his purpose was in the Garden of Eden. The Bible explains in Genesis 2:15:

*"The Lord God took the man and put him in the Garden of Eden to work it and take care of it."*

Man was given clear instructions: to work the garden and take care of it. According to the Strong's Hebrew-English Lexicon, the Hebrew word translated as "work" is "âḇaḏ," which means "to become." Therefore, man was told to become or reveal himself, doing what God created him to do—have dominion.

In addition to this instruction, God gave man an important commandment:

*"And the Lord God commanded the man, saying, 'Of every tree of the garden you may freely eat; but of the tree of the knowledge of good and evil you shall not eat, for in the day that you eat of it you shall surely die.'" — Genesis 2:16-17 (New King James Version, NKJV)*

Man was given a clear commandment: "but of the tree of the knowledge of good and evil you shall not eat." The consequence of disobedience was, *you shall surely die.*" However, man (Adam) disobeyed God and ate from the forbidden tree, prompted by his wife, Eve, who was deceived by the serpent, the devil.

*"Now the serpent was more subtle and crafty than any living creature of the field which the Lord God had made. And he [Satan] said to the woman, 'Can it really be that God has said, You shall not eat from every tree of the garden?' And the woman said to the serpent, 'We may eat the fruit from the trees of the garden, except the fruit from the tree which is in the middle of the garden. God has said, You shall not eat of it, neither shall you touch it, lest you die.' But the serpent said to the woman, 'You shall not surely die, for God knows that in the day you eat of it your eyes will be opened, and you will be like God, knowing the difference between good and evil and blessing and calamity.'" —Genesis 3:1-5 (Amplified Bible, Classic Edition, AMPC)*

From this passage, there are three important facts to note:

# 1. The Devil Had Insufficient Information

The devil asked Eve, *"...Can it really be that God has said, You shall not eat from every tree of the garden?"* —Genesis 3:1. God never said not to eat from every tree of the garden. God had said, *"Of every tree of the garden you may freely eat; but of the tree of the knowledge of good and evil you shall not eat..."* — Genesis 2:16-17. Therefore, God only commanded man not to eat from the tree of the knowledge of good and evil. It is clear from the Scriptures that the devil lacked complete information; he didn't know which specific tree man was commanded not to eat from, so he played on Eve's ignorance to get the information from her. However, the devil understood God's plan and purpose regarding the trees in the midst of the garden. How? Because the devil was once a beautiful angel named Lucifer who defied God and fell from grace, as described in Isaiah 14:12-15:

*"How you are fallen from heaven, O Lucifer, son of the morning! How you are cut down to the ground, You who weakened the nations! For you have said in your heart: 'I will ascend into heaven, I will exalt my throne above the stars of God; I will also sit on the mount of the*

*congregation on the farthest sides of the north; I will ascend above the heights of the clouds, I will be like the Most High.' Yet you shall be brought down to Sheol, to the lowest depths of the Pit." —New King James Version (NKJV)*

This background explains how the devil knew that the reason God commanded man not to eat from the tree of the knowledge of good and evil was because man would become like God, knowing the difference between good and evil:

*"But the serpent said to the woman, 'You shall not surely die, for God knows that in the day you eat of it your eyes will be opened, and you will be like God, knowing the difference between good and evil and blessing and calamity.'" —Genesis 3:4-5 (AMPC)*

So, the devil, in the form of a serpent, convinced Eve—who then convinced Adam—to eat the forbidden fruit from the tree of the knowledge of good and evil in the Garden of Eden, resulting in man's disobedience to God:

*"And when the woman saw that the tree was good (suitable, pleasant) for food and that it was delightful to*

*look at, and a tree to be desired in order to make one wise, she took of its fruit and ate; and she gave some also to her husband, and he ate. Then the eyes of them both were opened, and they knew that they were naked; and they sewed fig leaves together and made themselves apronlike girdles."* —Genesis 3:6-7 (AMPC)

After succumbing to the devil's deception, Adam and Eve were banished from the Garden of Eden and condemned to mortality:

*"But the Lord God called to Adam and said to him, 'Where are you?' He said, 'I heard the sound of You [walking] in the garden, and I was afraid because I was naked; and I hid myself.' And He said, 'Who told you that you were naked? Have you eaten of the tree of which I commanded you that you should not eat?' And the man said, 'The woman whom You gave to be with me—she gave me [fruit] from the tree, and I ate.' And the Lord God said to the woman, 'What is this you have done?' And the woman said, 'The serpent beguiled (cheated, outwitted, and deceived) me, and I ate.'"* —Genesis 3:9-13 (AMPC)

As a result, man was cursed and lost his privileged position to rule over the earth as a king.

Interestingly, there were two significant trees in the center of the Garden: the tree of life and the tree of the knowledge of good and evil:

*"The Lord God made all kinds of trees grow out of the ground—trees that were pleasing to the eye and good for food. In the middle of the garden were the tree of life and the tree of the knowledge of good and evil."* — Genesis 2:9 (NIV)

Yet, man chose to eat from the tree of the knowledge of good and evil. Why didn't man eat from the tree of life? Had he done so, man would have lived forever. How do we know this? Because God removed man from the garden to prevent him from eating from the tree of life:

*"Then the Lord God said, 'Behold, the man has become like one of Us, to know good and evil. And now, lest he put out his hand and take also of the tree of life, and eat, and live forever'— therefore the Lord God sent him out of the garden of Eden to till the ground from which he was taken."* —Genesis 3:22-23 (NIV)

Apparently, the tree of life was very important, both to God and to man. Therefore, God placed cherubim (celestial beings of the second order of angels) to guard the way to the tree of life with a flaming sword:

*"So He drove out the man; and He placed cherubim at the east of the garden of Eden, and a flaming sword which turned every way, to guard the way to the tree of life."* —Genesis 3:24 (NIV)

From these scriptures, it is clear that the reason God commanded man not to eat from the tree of the knowledge of good and evil was that man would become like God, capable of distinguishing between good and evil. The Bible states, "Then the Lord God said, 'Behold, the man has become like one of Us, to know good and evil.'" Who is the "Us" referred to in this scripture? The Amplified Bible, Classic Edition, provides the answer:

*"And the Lord God said, 'Behold, the man has become like one of Us [the Father, Son, and Holy Spirit], to know [how to distinguish between] good and evil and blessing and calamity; and now, lest he put forth his hand and*

*take also from the tree of life and eat, and live forever.'"*
—Genesis 3:22 (AMPC)

Therefore, it is clear that God did not place the trees in the midst of the garden to tempt man, as some critics suggest.

## 2. Eve Received the Instructions Not to Eat of the Forbidden Tree from Her Husband (Adam)

It is evident that Eve received the command not to eat from the forbidden tree from her husband, Adam. How do we know this? In Genesis 3:3, Eve tells the serpent, "God has said, 'You shall not eat of it, neither shall you touch it, lest you die.'" The truth is, God never explicitly said not to touch the tree; He only commanded Adam not to eat from it:

*"And the Lord God commanded the man, saying, 'Of every tree of the garden you may freely eat; but of the tree of the knowledge of good and evil you shall not eat, for in the day that you eat of it you shall surely die.'"* — Genesis 2:16-17 (NKJV)

Therefore, it is reasonable to conclude that Adam added the instruction "not to touch it" when relaying God's command to Eve. Additionally, Eve was not yet created when God gave the command to Adam. Genesis 2:18, and 21-23 outline the timeline:

*"Now the Lord God said, 'It is not good (sufficient, satisfactory) that the man should be alone; I will make him a helper (suitable, adapted, complementary) for him.' And the Lord God caused a deep sleep to fall upon Adam; and while he slept, He took one of his ribs or a part of his side and closed up the [place with] flesh. And the rib or part of his side which the Lord God had taken from the man He built up and made into a woman, and He brought her to the man. Then Adam said, 'This [creature] is now bone of my bones and flesh of my flesh; she shall be called Woman, because she was taken out of a man.'"* —Genesis 2:18, 21-23 (AMPC)

From these verses, we see that Eve was created in verses 21-22, after God had given the command to Adam in verses 16-17. This sequence confirms that the instruction Eve had about the forbidden tree likely came from Adam, further showing the importance of clear communication and the transmission of God's commands within relationships.

## 3. Adam Was Not Deceived

The Bible clearly states that Adam was not deceived, but rather, it was Eve who was deceived:

*"And it was not Adam who was deceived, but [the] woman who was deceived and deluded and fell into transgression."* —1 Timothy 2:14 (AMPC)

This distinction is crucial because it emphasizes that Adam acted with full knowledge of his disobedience. If Adam had been deceived, it would suggest that he lacked certain information and might imply that God was withholding something from him. However, this was not the case. Adam knew exactly why God had commanded him not to eat from the forbidden tree. He was not ignorant of God's plan and purpose concerning the trees in the midst of the garden.

God's instructions were clear, and there was no hidden agenda. The Bible affirms that everything God created was good:

*"And God saw everything that He had made, and behold, it was very good (suitable, pleasant) and He approved it completely."* —Genesis 1:31 (AMPC)

This statement includes the trees in the garden, which were also intended for man's benefit, though with divine timing and order. God even confirms that He provided every tree for food:

*"And God said, 'See, I have given you every plant yielding seed that is on the face of all the land and every tree with seed in its fruit; you shall have them for food.'"* —Genesis 1:29 (AMPC)

Thus, God created everything, including the trees, for man's good and not as a means to entrap or deceive him. Adam's decision to eat from the tree of the knowledge of good and evil, despite knowing the consequences, indicates a deliberate choice rather than deception.


## God's Intent to Train the Human Spirit

God intended for man to have dominion and rule as a king over the earth, but He also sought to train the human spirit to mature and handle such responsibilities wisely. The trees in the midst of the garden, particularly the tree of life and the tree of the knowledge of good and evil, were not meant as temptations but as part of God's greater plan for man's growth and development.

The Bible reveals that access to the tree of life is a privilege granted to those who overcome:

*"He who has an ear, let him hear what the Spirit says to the churches. To him who overcomes I will give to eat from the tree of life, which is in the midst of the Paradise of God."* —Revelation 2:7 (NKJV)

This indicates that partaking of the tree of life is reserved for those who demonstrate perseverance and faithfulness. The Amplified Bible expands on this, saying:

*"He who has an ear, let him hear and heed what the Spirit says to the churches. To him who overcomes [the world through believing that Jesus is the Son of God], I will grant [the privilege] to eat [the fruit] from the tree of life, which is in the Paradise of God."* —Revelation 2:7 (AMPC)

Thus, God's plan was not to withhold good things from man, but to prepare him to receive them in due time. The command not to eat from the tree of the knowledge of good and evil was part of this training process, teaching man obedience, trust, and reliance on God's timing.

Adam, with his understanding of God's will, knew that it was not yet time to eat from these trees. His transgression was not due to a lack of revelation or information but rather a willful act that went against the divine order set by God. This act led to the loss of his privileged position and a shift in the relationship between man and God. However, the promise of restoration through overcoming points to the ultimate redemption and the eventual access to the fullness of life that God originally intended for humanity.


## The Restoration of Man

The fall of man through disobedience brought separation from God, loss of dominion, and the curse of sin and death. However, from the very beginning, God had a plan for the restoration of humanity. This plan unfolds throughout the Bible, demonstrating God's relentless love, mercy, and grace towards His creation. The restoration of man is a profound journey from the depths of sin back to a position of righteousness, authority, and fellowship with God.

## 1. The Promise of Redemption

God's plan to restore man began immediately after the fall. In Genesis 3:15, often referred to as the protoevangelium or the "first gospel," God declared that the seed of the woman would crush the serpent's head:

*"And I will put enmity between you and the woman, and between your seed and her Seed; He shall bruise your head, and you shall bruise His heel."* —Genesis 3:15 (NKJV)

This prophetic declaration pointed to Jesus Christ, the ultimate Redeemer, who would defeat Satan and restore what was lost in the Garden of Eden. From this moment, God set in motion His redemptive plan, a promise that He would one day restore mankind to their rightful place.

## 2. The Sacrifice of Jesus Christ

The culmination of God's plan for the restoration of man is found in the person and work of Jesus Christ. God sent His only Son into the world to pay the price for sin and to restore humanity back to God. Jesus, being both fully God and fully man, lived a sinless life, fulfilling the law and the prophets. He willingly sacrificed Himself on the cross, taking upon Himself the sins of the world:

*"For God so loved the world that He gave His only begotten Son, that whoever believes in Him should not perish but have everlasting life."* —John 3:16 (NKJV)

Through His death, burial, and resurrection, Jesus conquered sin, death, and the grave. His resurrection is the cornerstone of the Christian faith and the guarantee of restoration for all who believe:

*"For if by the one man's offense death reigned through the one, much more those who receive abundance of grace and of the gift of righteousness will reign in life through the One, Jesus Christ."* —Romans 5:17 (NKJV)

## 3. The Restoration of Righteousness

Through faith in Jesus Christ, believers are justified and made righteous before God. This righteousness is not earned by works or human effort but is a gift from God, received through faith:

*"For He made Him who knew no sin to be sin for us, that we might become the righteousness of God in Him."* — 2 Corinthians 5:21 (NKJV)

This restoration of righteousness means that believers are no longer defined by their past sins or failures. Instead, they are seen as new creations in Christ, fully restored and made right with God:

*"Therefore, if anyone is in Christ, he is a new creation; old things have passed away; behold, all things have become new."* —2 Corinthians 5:17 (NKJV)

## 4. Restoration of Dominion and Kingship

Through Christ's redemptive work, believers are restored to their original position of authority and dominion. Jesus is described as the "King of kings," and as His followers, believers are called to reign in life:

*"...and has made us kings and priests to His God and Father, to Him be glory and dominion forever and ever. Amen."* —Revelation 1:6 (NKJV)

Believers are no longer slaves to sin or subject to the kingdom of darkness; they are transferred into the Kingdom of God, where they are empowered to walk in victory and authority:

*"He has delivered us from the power of darkness and conveyed us into the kingdom of the Son of His love."* — Colossians 1:13 (NKJV)

## 5. The Role of the Holy Spirit in Restoration

The Holy Spirit plays a crucial role in the restoration of man. Upon believing in Christ, believers are indwelt by the Holy Spirit, who empowers, guides, and transforms them into the image of Christ. The Holy Spirit is the seal of the believer's salvation and the guarantee of the full restoration to come:

*"In Him you also trusted, after you heard the word of truth, the gospel of your salvation; in whom also, having believed, you were sealed with the Holy Spirit of*

*promise, who is the guarantee of our inheritance until the redemption of the purchased possession, to the praise of His glory."* —Ephesians 1:13-14 (NKJV)

The Holy Spirit enables believers to live out their restored identity, providing the power to overcome sin, walk in righteousness, and fulfill God's purposes on earth.

## 6. The Ultimate Restoration: Eternal Life with God

The final aspect of restoration is the promise of eternal life with God. Believers are promised a future where they will dwell with God forever, free from sin, pain, and death. This ultimate restoration is described in Revelation:

*"And I heard a loud voice from heaven saying, 'Behold, the tabernacle of God is with men, and He will dwell with them, and they shall be His people. God Himself will be with them and be their God. And God will wipe away every tear from their eyes; there shall be no more death, nor sorrow, nor crying. There shall be no more pain, for the former things have passed away.'"* — Revelation 21:3-4 (NKJV)

Through Christ, believers are not only restored to their original purpose but are given a future that far exceeds what was lost in the fall. They are invited to reign with Christ for eternity, experiencing the fullness of life that God intended from the beginning.

# CHAPTER 2

# UNDERSTANDING YOUR ROYAL IDENTITY

## The Reality of Our Royal Status

As believers in Christ, it's vital to understand that we are not ordinary people. The moment we accepted Jesus as our Lord and Savior, we were transformed from mere mortals into kings in the Kingdom of God. This royal status is not just a lofty title; it is a profound reality that should shape every aspect of our lives.

The Bible tells us in Revelation 1:6 that God has *"made us kings and priests unto God and his Father; to him be glory and dominion for ever and ever. Amen."* This declaration is not just symbolic; it is a divine truth that defines who we are. As kings, we are endowed with authority, dominion, and the power to rule. However, many believers live far below their potential because they do not fully grasp this reality.

A king does not beg; he commands and makes decrees. He understands that his words carry weight and that his decrees have the power to shape his environment. In the same way, we, as spiritual kings, must move away from a mindset of lack, fear, and begging. Instead, we should embrace our royal identity and begin to live, speak, and act as kings.

## Understanding the Spiritual Kingdom

The Kingdom of God is a spiritual kingdom, and it operates by spiritual laws. Jesus said in John 18:36, *"My kingdom is not of this world..."* This statement emphasizes the spiritual nature of God's kingdom and the fact that it transcends the physical realm.

As citizens of this spiritual kingdom, our authority as kings is not derived from earthly status or possessions but from our position in Christ. The physical world is governed by the spiritual, and as kings, we are called to rule and reign from the spiritual realm. This means that our victories are first won in the spirit before they manifest in the physical.

Many believers struggle because they are too focused on the physical circumstances around them. They attempt to solve spiritual problems with physical solutions, which often leads to frustration and defeat. To live victoriously as a king, you must first secure your victories in the spirit. This requires a deep understanding of your identity in Christ and the spiritual authority that you possess.

Before anything manifests in the physical, it must first be received in the spirit. This is a fundamental principle of the Kingdom of God. Whether it's healing, provision, or breakthrough, it must be established in the spiritual realm before it becomes a reality in the natural.

In Mark 11:24, Jesus teaches us, *"Therefore I say unto you, What things soever ye desire, when ye pray, believe that ye receive them, and ye shall have them."* This scripture highlights the importance of receiving in the spirit first. The word "receive" here is translated from the Greek word "lambano," which means to take hold of, to seize, or to accept something as yours.

As kings, we must learn to operate from the spirit first. When you pray, see yourself already possessing what you've asked for. Accept it in your heart, confess it with your mouth, and then expect it to manifest in the physical. This is how kings operate—by faith, not by sight.

## The Life of God in Us

One of the most profound truths about our identity as kings is that we possess the very life of God within us. This life, referred to as "Zoe" in the Greek, is the God-kind of life. It is the life that empowers us to live above sickness, disease, poverty, and every form of defeat.

In John 10:10, Jesus declared, *"I am come that they might have life, and that they might have it more abundantly."* This abundant life is not just about material wealth or physical health; it is the very essence of God's nature dwelling within us. It is the life that causes us to reign as kings, to live in continuous victory, and to overcome every challenge that comes our way.

When you understand that the life of God is in you, you begin to see yourself differently. You no longer accept defeat, sickness, or lack as your portion. Instead, you speak life into every situation, knowing that the same power that raised Jesus from the dead lives in you (Romans 8:11). This consciousness of the life of God within us is what enables us to reign as kings in this life.

## The Origin of Our Kingship

Our kingship is not something we earned; it is a divine gift bestowed upon us by God. From the very beginning, God's intention was for humanity to rule and have dominion over the earth. In Genesis 1:26-28, God said, *"Let us make man in our image, after our likeness: and let them have dominion over the fish of the sea, and over the fowl of the air, and over the cattle, and over all the earth, and over every creeping thing that creepeth upon the earth."*

This dominion mandate was given to Adam, the first man, and through him, to all humanity. However, when Adam sinned, he lost this authority, and it was forfeited to Satan. But thanks be to God, through Jesus Christ, our dominion has been restored. Jesus, referred to as the "last Adam" (1 Corinthians 15:45), came to restore what was lost. Through His death and resurrection, He reinstated our authority and made us kings once again.

It is important to recognize that our kingship is rooted in God's original plan and purpose for humanity. It is not something we strive for; it is something we receive through Christ. Understanding this will give you the confidence to walk in your authority without hesitation, knowing that it is God's will for you to reign as a king.

## Understanding God's Nature

To fully embrace our identity as kings, we must understand the nature of the One who made us kings—God Himself. The Bible reveals that God is a God of abundance, prosperity, and excellence. In heaven, the streets are paved with gold, symbolizing the opulence and glory of God's Kingdom.

In Ephesians 3:20, Paul writes, *"Now unto him that is able to do exceeding abundantly above all that we ask or think, according to the power that worketh in us."* This scripture highlights the limitless nature of God's provision and His desire for us to live in abundance.

As kings, we are called to reflect God's nature in every area of our lives. This means living in excellence, walking in divine health, and experiencing prosperity in all things. It also means exercising authority over every situation, just as God exercises authority over the universe.

When you understand God's nature, you begin to see that lack, sickness, and defeat are not your portion. You realize that as a king, you are called to reign and to manifest God's nature in every aspect of your life. This understanding will empower you to walk in your kingship with confidence and authority, knowing that you are a reflection of the King of kings.

# CHAPTER 3

# EMBRACING YOUR ROYAL IDENTITY

The Bible reveals an extraordinary truth about our identity in Christ: *"Unto him that loved us, and washed us from our sins in his own blood, And hath made us kings and priests unto God and his Father; to him be glory and dominion forever and ever. Amen"* (Revelation 1:5-6). This passage underscores that as believers, we have been elevated to the status of kings and priests, a reality that transforms how we should perceive and conduct ourselves.

## You're Royalty

The moment you accepted Jesus Christ as your Lord and Savior, you were elevated to a status far above what the world can offer—you became royalty. This is not a symbolic statement or a metaphor; it is a spiritual reality grounded in the Word of God. Revelation 1:5-6 tells us, *"And from Jesus Christ, who is the faithful witness, and the first begotten of the dead, and the prince of the kings of the earth. Unto him that loved us, and washed us from our sins in his own blood, and hath made us kings and priests unto God and his Father; to him be glory and dominion for ever and ever. Amen."*

This passage reveals the extraordinary truth that we have been made kings and priests in God's Kingdom. This is not a status we earn or strive for; it is a gift that comes with being a child of God. As royalty, you are called to a life of authority, dominion, and influence. You are no longer subject to the circumstances of this world; rather, you are empowered to rule over them.

Understanding that you are royalty is the first step toward living a victorious Christian life. Many believers fail to walk in the fullness of their potential because they do not fully grasp their royal identity. They continue to live as though they are mere subjects of this world, begging for what has already been given to them. But once you recognize that you are a king, your perspective changes, and you begin to live with the confidence and authority that come with your royal status.

## The Royal Standard

The kings of the earth go to great lengths to raise their children with a sense of identity and responsibility because they are royalty. These children are groomed to represent their royal lineage; they walk, talk, dress, and behave differently from everyone else. The expectations are even higher for an heir-apparent, the one destined to inherit the throne.

Solomon, in reflecting on his upbringing, said, *"I was my father's son, tender and only beloved in the sight of my mother. He taught me also, and said unto me, Let thine heart retain my words: keep my commandments, and live"* (Proverbs 4:3-4). Although Solomon was not David's only child, he was the one specifically groomed for kingship. David imparted to him a special training and wisdom necessary for the throne, a privilege that was unique to Solomon.

Similarly, as God's children, we are not just ordinary people; we are His heirs. *"And if children, then heirs;*

*heirs of God, and joint-heirs with Christ..."* (Romans 8:17). This means that everything God has belong to us, and we share in the inheritance with Jesus Christ. Understanding this truth changes everything about how we live and interact with the world around us.

As a member of God's royal family, you are held to a higher standard. Just as earthly royalty is expected to live, speak, and act in a manner befitting their status, so too are we as spiritual royalty expected to uphold the standards of God's Kingdom. The Bible says in 1 Peter 2:9, *"But ye are a chosen generation, a royal priesthood, an holy nation, a peculiar people; that ye should shew forth the praises of him who hath called you out of darkness into his marvellous light."*

This scripture highlights the fact that we are not just royalty; we are a royal priesthood, set apart to demonstrate the glory and excellence of God. This means that our lives should reflect the character and nature of God in everything we do. We are called to live above reproach, to walk in love, and to display the fruits of the Spirit in every aspect of our lives.

The royal standard also involves understanding the responsibilities that come with our position. As royalty, we are not just called to enjoy the benefits of our status; we are also called to be stewards of God's Kingdom on earth. This means using our influence and authority to bring about God's will in our lives, in the lives of others, and in the world around us. It means living a life that is worthy of the calling we have received, knowing that we represent the King of kings in everything we do.

## Walking in Royalty

You are not an ordinary person; you are royalty. Your Heavenly Father, the Creator and owner of the entire universe, has placed you in charge of His possessions. *"All things are yours"* (1 Corinthians 3:21), declares the Bible, highlighting the immense honor and responsibility that comes with being an heir of God.

As royalty, you've been called to reign in life. This isn't just a symbolic title; it's a call to live, walk, and talk like the king that you are. Refuse to engage in cheap talk or live a beggarly life. Kings don't beg; they exercise authority. They speak with power and confidence, knowing that their words carry weight.

Even in your prayers, approach God with the confidence of a son who knows his Father loves him and has given him access to an inexhaustible inheritance. You don't need to beg; you simply declare what is rightfully yours as an heir of God. This is the mindset and lifestyle of royalty.

To walk in royalty means to live consciously aware of your identity as a king in God's Kingdom. It is not enough to know that you are royalty; you must also walk in it. This involves aligning your thoughts, words, and actions with your royal status. Romans 5:17 declares, *"For if by one man's offence death reigned by one; much more they which receive abundance of grace and of the gift of righteousness shall reign in life by one, Jesus Christ."*

Walking in royalty means reigning in life through the grace and righteousness that have been given to you in Christ. It means taking your place of authority and using it to overcome challenges, resist the devil, and manifest the Kingdom of God in every area of your life.

It involves a mindset shift—from seeing yourself as a victim to seeing yourself as a victor, from living in fear to living in faith, from begging for blessings to commanding them.

One of the key aspects of walking in royalty is understanding the power of your words. Ecclesiastes 8:4 says, *"Where the word of a king is, there is power: and who may say unto him, What doest thou?"* As a king, your words carry weight; they have the power to shape your reality and to bring God's will into manifestation. When you speak, speak with the authority that comes from knowing who you are in Christ. Declare God's promises over your life and watch as they come to pass.

Walking in royalty also means walking in confidence. Confidence is not arrogance; it is the assurance that comes from knowing that God is with you, that He has empowered you, and that He has given you everything you need to succeed. When you walk in royalty, you walk with your head held high, knowing that you are a child of the King and that no weapon formed against you shall prosper.

## Embrace Your Royal Identity

As you meditate on these truths, let the reality of your royal status in Christ permeate your heart and mind. You are not just a follower of Christ; you are a king, called to rule and reign in life. Your words, actions, and mindset should reflect this royal identity. Speak with authority, live with purpose, and walk in the fullness of your inheritance in Christ.

Embracing your royal identity is about fully accepting and living out the reality of who you are in Christ. It means rejecting any thoughts, beliefs, or behaviors that are inconsistent with your royal status. It means renewing your mind with the Word of God until you see yourself as God sees you—as a king, a conqueror, and a victor in every situation.

Romans 12:2 urges us, *"And be not conformed to this world: but be ye transformed by the renewing of your mind, that ye may prove what is that good, and acceptable, and perfect, will of God."* To embrace your royal identity, you must renew your mind daily with the truth of God's Word. This involves meditating on scriptures that affirm your identity in Christ, speaking them over your life, and acting on them in faith.

Embracing your royal identity also means letting go of the past. The enemy will often try to remind you of your past failures, mistakes, and shortcomings to keep you from walking in your royal identity. But the Bible says in 2 Corinthians 5:17, *"Therefore if any man be in Christ, he is a new creature: old things are passed away; behold, all things are become new."* As a new creation in Christ, you are no longer defined by your past; you are defined by who you are in Christ.

Finally, embracing your royal identity means living with a sense of purpose and destiny. As royalty, you are not here by accident; you have been called to fulfill a divine purpose. God has a plan for your life, and it is a plan of good, not of evil, to give you a future and a hope (Jeremiah 29:11). When you embrace your royal identity, you begin to walk in the purpose that God has for you, and you experience the fullness of His blessings in your life.

# CHAPTER 4

# UNDERSTANDING DECREES

To fully grasp the power and significance of decrees within a biblical context, it is essential to first understand what a decree is. This chapter will explore the definition of a decree from various perspectives, including its secular usage, governmental implications, and most importantly, its divine and biblical significance.

## What is a Decree?

According to two online dictionaries, dictionary.com and yourdictionary.com, a decree is defined as:

1. An official order, edict, or decision issued by a church, government, court, etc.

2. An authoritative order having the force of law, such as a presidential decree.

3. An edict, law, or regulation made by someone in authority.

4. In law, an order or judgment of a court made after hearing a suit, especially in matrimonial proceedings.

5. In theology, one of the eternal purposes of God, by which events are foreordained.

6. To command, ordain, or decide by decree.

From these definitions, for something to be called a decree, it must have the following elements:

- It must be a decision—you must have decided on what you want.

- It must have the force of law.

- It must be made by someone in authority or who has authority.

- It must align with the purposes of God.

- It must be a command or must be authoritative.

Therefore, a decree can be an order, law, judgment, edict, or decision. The six dictionary definitions encompass both legal and theological perspectives. To fully understand what a decree is, I will explain it in the context of both secular and Biblical definitions.

**Authority Behind a Decree**

You cannot make a decree without having the authority to do so. A decree is an edict, law, or decision made by someone in authority. It must also be backed by the law, and the decree must be enforceable by that law. The power of the law enforces the decree to be established. To make a decree is to issue an authoritative order with the force of law, empowering its establishment.

For example, in legal terms, a decree is an order or judgment of a court made by a judge after hearing a suit, such as in matrimonial proceedings. A judge can issue a decree because they have the authority to do so, and the decree is established due to the backing of the power or force of the law. Decrees are typically enforced, and if not upheld, those who break them are punished under the same law by which they were enacted. This means there are consequences, and the severity of the punishment aligns with the level of the decree violated.

Similarly, a decree is an official order, edict, or decision issued by a church, government, or court. For instance, governments often make decrees for the entire population within their jurisdiction. Governments have the authority to make these decrees and the power to enforce them. Those who refuse to obey these decrees are subject to the punishments or judgments of governmental authorities. For example, in most nations, governments decree that all citizens must pay taxes, which is obligatory. If a citizen breaks this decree, they are punished under the law based on the decree's terms.

## God's Decrees

A decree is also one of the eternal purposes of God, by which events are foreordained. These are decrees enacted by God that enforce His purposes and will on earth for mankind. These decrees are eternal and, as such, are unbreakable. For instance, God decreed in Isaiah 46:9-10 (ESV):

*"...for I am God, and there is no other; I am God, and there is none like me, declaring the end from the beginning and from ancient times things not yet done, saying, 'My counsel shall stand, and I will accomplish all my purpose.'"*

This decree declares God's sovereignty, stating that He alone has supreme power and authority over all the earth. God has the authority to make this declaration because He is the Almighty, the Creator of the earth and the universe:

*"The earth is the Lord's, and all its fullness, the world and those who dwell therein." —Psalm 24:1 (NKJV)*

Through this decree, God declares that "My counsel shall stand, and I will accomplish all my purpose." Here, "counsel" means purpose, and as stated in the Amplified Bible, *"My purpose will be established, And I will do all that pleases Me and fulfills My purpose."* This is why He boldly decrees that through His Son, Jesus Christ, we can be forgiven of our sins and be declared righteous in His sight:

*"For God made Christ, who never sinned, to be the offering for our sin, so that we could be made right with God through Christ."* —2 Corinthians 5:21 (NLT)

This is significant because God has the authority to declare that if a person accepts His Son, Jesus Christ, as Lord and Savior and believes in His name, they are declared righteous (in right standing with God). Therefore, salvation is not about what a person has done or should do but purely about what Christ has done. Humanity is made right with God because Jesus Christ offered Himself as a sin offering for the remission of sin. As such, there is no alternative for salvation:

*"And there is salvation in no one else; for there is no other name under heaven that has been given among people by which we must be saved [for God has provided the world no alternative for salvation]."* —Acts 4:12 (Amplified Bible)

However, just as with any decree—such as those issued by governments—those who refuse to obey God's decrees are subject to His judgment if they do not accept Jesus Christ as their personal Lord and Savior by believing in His name and His work for the remission of sins. God has appointed that man is destined to die once and afterward face judgment:

*"And just as it is appointed and destined for all men to die once and after this [comes certain] judgment," —* Hebrews 9:27 (Amplified Bible)

This is a decree from God, and it is unchangeable. Every person will die and face God's judgment. This also applies to anyone alive at the second coming of Christ, when the world ends, as outlined in Revelation 20:12-15:

*"And I saw the dead, the great and the small, standing before the throne, and books were opened. Then another book was opened, which is the Book of Life; and the dead were judged according to what they had done as written in the books [that is, everything done while on earth]. And the sea gave up the dead who were in it, and death and Hades (the realm of the dead) surrendered the dead who were in them; and they were judged and sentenced, every one according to their deeds. Then death and Hades [the realm of the dead] were thrown into the lake of fire. This is the second death, the lake of fire [the*

*eternal separation from God]. And if anyone's name was not found written in the Book of Life, he was hurled into the lake of fire." —Amplified Bible*

The difference between decrees made by a church, government, or court and God's decrees is that God's decrees can never be revoked:

*"He set them in place forever and ever. His decree will never be revoked." —Psalm 148:6 (NLT)*

## Types of Decree

### Secular Definition of Decree

In its most basic form, a decree is an authoritative order that has the force of law. It is a command issued by a person or body with legal authority, such as a government, a court, or a ruler. A decree can be likened to a judicial decision or an official edict, which must be followed by those under its jurisdiction.

For example, in the secular world, a court might issue a decree in the form of a ruling that must be obeyed by all parties involved. Failure to adhere to such a decree can result in legal consequences, such as fines, imprisonment, or other forms of punishment. In this context, a decree is not just a suggestion; it is a binding order that demands compliance.

This secular understanding of a decree is crucial because it sets the stage for understanding the weight and authority that a decree carries, whether it is issued by a government, a court, or, as we will see, by God Himself.

## Governmental Decree

Governments often utilize decrees to govern and manage their populations. A governmental decree is an official order that is administered and enforced by the ruling authorities, and it is typically applied to all citizens within that government's jurisdiction.

A classic biblical example of a governmental decree is found in the account of the Roman census, where *"a decree went out from Caesar Augustus that all the world should be registered"* (Luke 2:1). This decree required citizens to return to their place of origin to be counted, an act that was mandatory and had legal implications. The Roman government, with its authority, enforced this decree, and failure to comply could result in severe penalties.

Governmental decrees, therefore, are powerful tools used by authorities to implement policies, enforce laws, and maintain order. They are binding and non-negotiable, reflecting the governing body's power and control over its subjects.

## God's Decree

Moving from the secular and governmental realms, we now turn to the most significant form of a decree: God's decree. In the Bible, God's decrees are divine commands that are both sovereign and eternal. Unlike human decrees, which can be challenged or revoked, God's decrees are unchangeable and must come to pass.

God's decrees encompass His will and purpose for creation, history, and humanity. They are often revealed through His word and carried out through His power. For instance, in the creation narrative, God decreed the existence of light, land, seas, and living creatures, and these came into being through the power of His spoken word. His decree was not just a command but a creative act that brought forth reality from nothingness.

In the New Testament, we see the ultimate expression of God's decree in His plan for redemption through Jesus Christ. Paul writes about this divine decree in 1 Corinthians 2:7, stating, *"But we speak the wisdom of God in a mystery, the hidden wisdom which God ordained before the ages for our glory."* This decree of redemption, hidden for ages, was manifested in Christ's death and resurrection, a plan that no power or authority could overturn.

God's decrees are not just expressions of His will; they are the execution of His sovereign plan, and they encompass all of creation. From the fall of man to the final judgment, everything unfolds according to God's decreed will.

## Disaster Decree

While God's decrees often bring about creation, blessing, and redemption, they can also include judgments and decrees of disaster against those who persist in disobedience. The Bible contains numerous instances where God decreed disaster as a consequence of sin and rebellion.

For example, in Jeremiah 11:17, we see God's decree of disaster against the nations of Israel and Judah due to their idolatry and disobedience: *"The Lord of hosts who planted you has decreed disaster against you because of the evil that the house of Israel and the house of Judah have done, provoking me to anger by making offerings to Baal."* This decree was a direct result of the people's persistent sin and served as a warning of the serious consequences of turning away from God.

Such decrees of disaster demonstrate that God's decrees are not only acts of creation and blessing but also instruments of divine justice. They remind us that God is holy and just, and His decrees serve to uphold His righteousness, even when it means bringing judgment.

## Unrighteous Decrees

In addition to righteous decrees issued by God, the Bible also warns against unrighteous decrees made by human rulers and authorities. These are decrees that promote injustice, oppression, and evil, often made by those who abuse their power.

Isaiah 10:1-2 provides a stark condemnation of such decrees: "*Woe to those who decree iniquitous decrees, and the writers who keep writing oppression, to turn aside the needy from justice and to rob the poor of my people of their right, that widows may be their spoil, and that they may make the fatherless their prey.*" These unrighteous decrees are in direct opposition to God's will and are condemned by Him.

Unrighteous decrees highlight the danger of human authority when it is exercised apart from God's justice and righteousness. They serve as a warning that while humans may issue decrees with the intent to oppress, God's ultimate justice will prevail, and those who enact such decrees will be held accountable.

## Does Man Have the Ability to Make Decrees?

As established in the previous chapter, only the restored or redeemed man has the power to make decrees because he has been made a king and has the authority of a king. The question is: What does the

Bible say about decrees, and how can the redeemed man use his kingship authority to make them?

Regarding your authority (if you are a restored or redeemed man) to make decrees, God says in Job 22:28:

*"You will also decree a thing, and it will be established for you; And light will shine on your ways." —New American Standard Bible (NASB)*

Therefore, the redeemed man has been given the authority to make decrees. A decree is an order or a decision, which means it is your decision to make them. If you choose not to make decrees, God will not make them for you. You must decide what you want to see happen in your world and make the decrees for it to occur. This is emphasized in the Amplified Bible, Classic Edition, which renders this Scripture as, *"You shall also decide and decree a thing, and it shall be established for you; and the light [of God's favor] shall shine upon your ways."* What you do not decree cannot be established for you. If you decree nothing, nothing will be established for you.

## How to Make Decrees

Decrees are made through declarations. The English dictionary defines declaration as a formal announcement, statement, or proclamation. The New King James Version renders Job 22:28 as, *"You will also declare a thing, And it will be established for you; So light will shine on your ways."* In essence, you make decrees by declaring what you want to see happen in your life and in your world.

A common concern among Christians is: What if I make decrees and nothing happens? That is not for you to worry about because it is not your responsibility to bring them to pass—that is God's responsibility. The Bible says in Isaiah 44:26:

*"[The Lord] Who confirms the word of His servant and performs the counsel of His messengers, Who says of Jerusalem, She shall [again] be inhabited, and of the cities of Judah, They shall [again] be built, and I will raise up their ruins." —Amplified Bible, Classic Edition (AMPC)*

God's role is to confirm the word of His servant and fulfill the counsel of His messengers. As long as you are a redeemed child of God, you are His servant and messenger. You do not need to be a pastor, evangelist, or prophet to be God's servant or messenger. So, do your part and leave God's part for Him to do. Why are you worrying for God? Are you a deputy God? And for your information, God has no deputy. This is one of the reasons why many make decrees that are not established—stop worrying about God's part. He doesn't need your help; He is the Almighty God. He says, *"Behold, I am the Lord, the God of all flesh. Is there anything too hard for Me?"* —Jeremiah 3:27 (NKJV).

All you need to do is believe Him, for *"...blessed is she that believed: for there shall be a performance of those things..."* —Luke 1:45 (KJV). If He said, *"I will confirm the word of my servant and perform the counsel of my messengers,"* then trust Him to do it, for God cannot lie. He affirmed this truth in Isaiah 55:11:

*"So shall My word be that goes forth from My mouth; It shall not return to Me void, But it shall accomplish what I please, And it shall prosper in the thing for which I sent it."* —New King James Version (NKJV)

In the words of a songwriter, "God said it, I believe it, and that settles it"—this should be your stance.

## The Power of the Tongue in Making Decrees

However, great care must be taken when making a decree. Consider carefully what you want to decree, decide if it is truly what you desire, and ensure you wish to make the decree before doing so. This is important because there is power in your tongue:

*"Death and life are in the power of the tongue, and they who indulge in it shall eat the fruit of it [for death or life]."* —Proverbs 18:21 (Amplified Bible, Classic Edition)

Be mindful of your words, for death and life are in the power of the tongue, and you will experience its outcomes—whether good or bad, life or death. Remember, you will decree a thing, and it will be established for you. When you make a decree, you are declaring with the weight of God's authority behind it. Your decree is also a prophetic and authoritative word that has the power to unlock the supernatural and cause a shift in both the spiritual and physical realms.

## The Prophetic Nature of Decrees

Lastly, your decree is prophetic when it is sourced in God's Word. A decree involves taking God's words and speaking them out. With the authority you have on earth as a king, you can enforce God's plans and purposes through the agreement of your own words. Jesus Christ has given you this authority to make decrees into your realms of influence. As you do so, you begin to create the will of God in your life in the spiritual realm, which will ultimately manifest in the physical realm, for God has said:

*"By me kings reign, And rulers decree justice."* — *Proverbs 8:15 (NKJV)*

This is a new day for you. You are blessed.

## Decree and Proclamation

In simple terms, a decree is an official order, edict, or decision that carries the force of law, while a proclamation is an announcement or the act of officially announcing something. Decrees are typically followed by proclamations, forming a two-step process: first, the decree is made, and second, the decree is officially announced through a proclamation.

Even in the Bible, royal decrees were followed by proclamations. It was not enough for a king or ruler to simply make a decree; the decree had to be publicized and conveyed throughout the kingdom via proclamation. This announcement was crucial because it enabled people to respond and position themselves to obey the decree. Without the official announcement, citizens of the kingdom might remain unaware of the decree. Therefore, it's important to understand that decrees and proclamations work hand in hand.

Similarly, it is not enough for us to make decrees during private prayers and intercession; we must also announce or pronounce these decrees publicly. However, there is still power in decrees made in private prayer and intercession.

When we decree what we want to see in the future, it is referred to as a prophetic decree. Likewise, a prophetic decree requires a prophetic proclamation. Prophetic decrees and proclamations are particularly powerful when used together, which is why many prophetic leaders—such as Prophets, Apostles, and Pastors—make prophetic declarations in their meetings. By making these declarations, they are engaging in public prophetic proclamation, thereby announcing the prophetic decrees.

This is why prophetic ministering is a powerful way of preaching God's Word, unveiling and enforcing God's purposes on earth and in the lives of His people. It enables God's people to position themselves for and respond to their Father's intentions, desires, and purposes through prophetic proclamation. As Scripture rightly says:

*"You will also decree a thing, and it will be established for you; And light will shine on your ways."* —Job 22:28 (New American Standard Bible, NASB)

## The Divine Decree and Its Importance

In conclusion, the concept of a decree, whether secular, governmental, or divine, carries with it a profound weight of authority and power. While secular and governmental decrees are important in maintaining order and governance, they pale in comparison to the divine decrees of God, which are eternal, unchangeable, and sovereign.

Understanding God's decrees are crucial for believers because they reveal the nature of God's will and His sovereign plan for humanity. God's decrees are not just historical events recorded in Scripture; they are living realities that continue to shape the world today. Whether they bring about creation, blessing, judgment, or justice, God's decrees are the ultimate expression of His authority and power.

As we move forward in this book, we will explore how believers can tap into the power of decrees, particularly prophetic decrees, to align their lives with God's will, declare His purposes, and experience the fullness of His Kingdom on earth.

# CHAPTER 5

# POWER IN THE WORD

## The Creative Force of Words

From the very beginning of time, the power of words has been foundational to the creation and shaping of reality. In Genesis, we see that God spoke the world into existence: *"And God said, 'Let there be light,' and there was light"* (Genesis 1:3). This divine act of creation through spoken words is not merely a historical account; it is a powerful truth that reverberates through time and space, impacting our lives today.

As beings created in God's image, we share in this divine attribute. Our words carry the same creative force that brought the universe into being. This is not just a spiritual truth but also resonates with the principles of quantum physics, where vibrations and energy are understood to influence the physical world. When we speak, we release energy into the atmosphere—energy that has the potential to create, transform, and manifest realities.

## The Power of Intentional Speech

Given the immense power that words hold, it is crucial for us to be intentional about what we speak. Proverbs 18:21 tells us, *"Death and life are in the power of the tongue: and they that love it shall eat the fruit thereof."* This scripture underscores that our words can bring either life or death, blessings or curses, into our lives and the lives of others. The words we speak are not just fleeting sounds; they are seeds that produce fruit— either good or bad.

We must be deliberate about the words we speak, aligning our speech with the promises of God and speaking life, success, health, and abundance into our circumstances. Understanding that the Word of God can change our reality transforms how we engage with it. Reading and memorizing scripture becomes an act of excitement, not obligation, because we recognize it as a powerful tool for creating the future we desire.

## Words and Decrees

Words matter—immensely. They hold the power to create life or death. As believers, we must be vigilant about what we say, especially when speaking over ourselves and others. Negative self-talk, doubt, and fear-based declarations can manifest unwanted realities in our lives. Phrases like "I am bad at...," "I can't...," "I always fail...," "I am worried...," or "I don't want this to happen..." are not merely expressions of concern; they are declarations that can set the stage for failure, fear, and anxiety.

The key is to stop negative speech and replace it with declarations that align with God's promises. Instead of focusing on what you don't want, speak what you do want. Declare your identity in Christ, your victory, your health, your prosperity, and your peace. The Bible is not just a book to be read—it is alive, and there is true power in speaking it out loud. When we speak God's

Word, we release its power into our lives, bringing about transformation and change.

## The Creative Power of God's Word

God demonstrated the ultimate power of words by creating the world through them. His Word is the original creative force, and as His children, we are called to use our words to create, bless, and build up. Hebrews 4:12 affirms that *the word of God is quick, and powerful, and sharper than any two-edged sword.*" This means that the Word is not just informative but transformative, capable of cutting through circumstances and bringing about God's will on earth.

Every time we speak scripture, we are not merely reciting words; we are unleashing the same creative power that God used to bring the universe into existence. We are partnering with God to bring His Kingdom to earth, to see His will done in our lives and the lives of those around us.

## Practical Application: Speaking Scripture and Decrees

I am passionate about speaking scripture and making decrees over every area of my life. There is something powerful about declaring God's Word with your own voice. Below are some areas of life where I consistently speak scriptures and make decrees:

- **Health:** *"By His stripes, I am healed"* (Isaiah 53:5). I decree that I walk in divine health, free from sickness and disease.

- **Finances:** *"The Lord is my shepherd; I shall not want"* (Psalm 23:1). I decree that my needs are met, and I live in abundance.

- **Peace:** *"The peace of God, which surpasses all understanding, will guard your hearts and minds through Christ Jesus"* (Philippians 4:7). I decree that I am filled with God's peace, regardless of my circumstances.

- **Success:** *"I can do all things through Christ who strengthens me"* (Philippians 4:13). I decree that I am successful in all my endeavors, for God is with me.

These are not just empty words; they are powerful declarations that align my life with God's will and release His power to bring about the desired outcomes. I encourage you to find scriptures that speak to your situation and begin to decree them over your life with boldness and faith. Remember, the Word is alive, and it has the power to change your reality.

The power in the Word is not just a theological concept but a practical tool for living a victorious life. By speaking God's Word and making decrees based on His promises, we align ourselves with His will and release His power to work in our lives. Let us be intentional with our words, knowing that they carry the power to create the life God has destined for us.

# CHAPTER 6

# THE POWER AND IMPACT OF DECREES AND DECLARATIONS

Decrees, when spoken with faith and authority, carry the power to transform not only the spiritual atmosphere but also the physical world. This chapter delves into the profound impact that decrees can have on various aspects of life, exploring the biblical foundation, spiritual significance, and even the science behind the spoken word.

## The Knowledge of Your Kingship

The foundation of walking in the authority of a king is rooted in the knowledge of your kingship in Christ. Before you can effectively make decrees and see them established, you must first understand who you are.

The Bible is clear about our identity as believers. In Revelation 1:6, it says, *"And hath made us kings and priests unto God and his Father; to him be glory and dominion for ever and ever. Amen."* This scripture reveals that we are not merely followers of Christ; we are kings in His Kingdom.

Just as an heir who is unaware of his inheritance is no different from a servant, a child of God who does not understand his royal status will live below his potential. Galatians 4:1 illustrates this truth: *"...the heir, as long as he is a child, differeth nothing from a servant, though he be lord of all."* It is not enough to merely know you are a king; this knowledge must become a core part of your mindset. You must think, speak, and act as a king, knowing that you are called to reign in life through Christ Jesus.

Knowing your kingship is crucial because it shapes your mindset and approach to life. A king does not beg or plead for what is rightfully his. He understands that he has been given authority to rule and to decree what should be. Similarly, as a spiritual king, you must know that you have been given authority by God to make decrees and to see those decrees come to pass. This knowledge is what empowers you to walk in dominion, knowing that all of heaven backs the words you speak in faith.

In addition to understanding your kingship, it's important to recognize that this kingship is not something you earned or achieved on your own. It is a gift from God, a position that He has placed you in through Jesus Christ. Romans 5:17 declares, *"For if by one man's offence death reigned by one; much more they which receive abundance of grace and of the gift of righteousness shall reign in life by one, Jesus Christ."* This means that your ability to reign as a king is not dependent on your own efforts but on the grace and righteousness that have been given to you in Christ. Your calling as a king is not just a title; it is a mandate to reign, to exercise dominion and authority in every area of your life.

## The Power of a King's Word

The words of a king carry immense power. Ecclesiastes 8:4 states, *"Where the word of a king is, there is power: and who may say unto him, What doest thou?"* This scripture underscores the authority that a king's words possess. When a king speaks, his words are not mere suggestions or wishes; they are commands that must be obeyed. In the same way, as a spiritual king, your words carry the authority of heaven, and they have the power to bring about change in your life and circumstances.

The Bible emphasizes the power of words in many places. Proverbs 18:21 tells us, *"Death and life are in the power of the tongue: and they that love it shall eat the fruit thereof."* This means that the words you speak can either bring life or death, blessings or curses. As a king, you must be intentional about the words you speak, knowing that your declarations have the power to shape your reality.

When you make decrees as a king, you are not speaking empty words; you are releasing the power of God into your situation. Job 22:28 says, *"Thou shalt also decree a thing, and it shall be established unto thee: and the light shall shine upon thy ways."* This scripture is a powerful reminder that when you decree something in faith, it will be established. The light of God's favor and blessing will shine upon your ways, bringing about the manifestation of what you have declared.

To fully harness the power of your words, it's important to align your declarations with the Word of God. The Bible is the ultimate authority, and when you speak in agreement with it, you are releasing the power of God's Word into your life. Isaiah 55:11 says, *"So shall my word be that goeth forth out of my mouth: it shall not return unto me void, but it shall accomplish that which I please, and it shall prosper in the thing whereto I sent it."* This means that when you speak God's Word, it will accomplish what it was sent to do.

Your words are not just empty phrases; they are powerful tools that can shape your reality. This understanding should transform your prayer life. Instead of begging or pleading, you are called to exercise your authority in Christ Jesus. You are not to approach God as a beggar but as a king who understands his rights and privileges in the Kingdom.

## Reject the Mentality of Begging

One of the biggest hindrances to walking in your kingship is a mentality of begging. Many believers approach God as beggars, pleading for what has already been provided for them in Christ. However, this is not the mindset of a king. A king does not beg; he makes decrees. He understands that everything he needs has already been made available to him, and he exercises his authority to bring it into manifestation.

Begging is a sign of unbelief and a lack of understanding of your identity in Christ. When you beg, you are essentially saying that you are unsure whether God will provide for you or fulfill His promises. But the Bible says in 2 Peter 1:3, *"According as his divine power hath given unto us all things that pertain unto life and godliness, through the knowledge of him that hath called us to glory and virtue."* This means that God has already given you everything you need for life and godliness. You don't need to beg; you need to take hold of what is already yours by faith.

Many Christians fall into the habit of begging—whether it's begging for health, financial provision, or even God's help. This mindset is not only unproductive but also contrary to the identity of a king. When you beg for what is already rightfully yours in Christ, you undermine the authority that has been given to you.

Understand this: It was not your request or idea that made you a king; it was God's divine decision. He chose to elevate you to this position of authority, and your response should be to live out your kingship. You have been given authority over Satan, sickness, disease, and every negative circumstance. As a king, you are to command situations to align with God's Word.

To reject the mentality of begging, you must renew your mind with the Word of God. Romans 12:2 instructs us, *"And be not conformed to this world: but be ye transformed by the renewing of your mind, that ye may prove what is that good, and acceptable, and perfect, will of God."* As you renew your mind, you begin to see yourself as God sees you—as a king who has been given authority to decree and to command things to come into alignment with God's will.

Instead of begging, begin to make declarations of faith. Speak what you desire to see in your life, knowing that your words have the power to bring it into existence. Declare God's promises over your health, your finances, your family, and every area of your life. As you do, you will see the manifestation of God's blessings, and you will walk in the fullness of your kingship.

## Exercising Your Authority

As a king, you have been given authority to rule and to reign in life. This authority is not something you need to earn or strive for; it is a gift that has been given to you through Jesus Christ. Luke 10:19 says, *"Behold, I give unto you power to tread on serpents and scorpions, and over all the power of the enemy: and nothing shall by any means hurt you."* This verse highlights the authority you have been given over all the power of the enemy.

Exercising your authority involves speaking to situations and commanding them to align with God's Word. Whether it's a health issue, a financial challenge, or a difficult relationship, you have the authority to speak to it and to command it to change. Mark 11:23

says, *"For verily I say unto you, That whosoever shall say unto this mountain, Be thou removed, and be thou cast into the sea; and shall not doubt in his heart, but shall believe that those things which he saith shall come to pass; he shall have whatsoever he saith."* This scripture shows the power of speaking in faith and the authority you have to command mountains—symbolic of obstacles and challenges—to move.

Exercising your authority also involves resisting the devil and his schemes. James 4:7 says, *"Submit yourselves therefore to God. Resist the devil, and he will flee from you."* As a king, you are not to tolerate the works of the enemy in your life. You have the authority to resist him and to command him to flee. Use your authority to bind and to loose, to cast out demons, and to declare God's will over your life.

If there's a growth in your body, command it to dematerialize in the Name of Jesus. If there's a challenging situation at work, school, or home, decree the outcome you desire according to God's promises, and it shall be so. Your authority in Christ is real and powerful; use it to shape your life according to God's will.

As you meditate on these scriptures and embrace your identity as a king, remember that your words carry divine authority. Speak life, decree God's will, and watch as His Kingdom is established in every area of your life. Kings don't beg; they make decrees.

In addition to speaking and resisting, exercising your authority means living in the confidence that comes from knowing that you are a king. It means walking with the assurance that God has your back, that He is with you, and that He has empowered you to reign in life. As you exercise your authority, you will see the Kingdom of God manifested in your life, and you will walk in the victory that God has ordained for you.

## The Power of Your Prophetic Decree

The concept of decrees in the Bible takes on a new dimension when we consider the prophetic nature of certain decrees. Unlike general declarations or statements of truth, prophetic decrees are specific, authoritative commands spoken in alignment with God's revealed will. This chapter explores the depth of prophetic decrees, their power, and their impact on both the spiritual and natural realms.

A prophetic decree is more than just a spoken word; it is an authoritative declaration that carries the weight of the Kingdom of God. When we make a prophetic decree, we are not merely stating our desires or opinions. Instead, we are aligning our words with God's will, as revealed to us through the Holy Spirit, and speaking them into existence with divine authority.

The Bible provides several examples of prophetic decrees that have shaped the course of history. For instance, in the book of Ezra, King Cyrus issued a decree to rebuild the temple in Jerusalem, which was backed by the resources of the Persian Empire (Ezra 1:1-4). This decree was prophetic because it aligned with God's plan for His people and led to the fulfillment of His purposes.

In essence, a prophetic decree is a divine order issued on earth by God's representatives—His sons and daughters—who have the authority to enforce the Father's will. This authority comes from our position in

Christ, who has given us the power to bind and loose on earth as it is in heaven (Matthew 18:18). When we speak a prophetic decree, we are not just expressing a wish or hope; we are commanding circumstances to align with God's established will.

## Prophetic Decree as a Standpoint, Not a Formula

It's important to differentiate between a prophetic decree and a formulaic approach to declarations. A key aspect of the power of prophetic decrees is recognizing that they are a standpoint rather than a formula. The power of a prophetic decree does not lie in the specific words used or the repetition of a phrase, but in the alignment of the decree with God's revealed will.

A formula implies a set of prescribed words or actions that, when followed, guarantee a specific outcome. However, prophetic decrees are not about following a script. They are dynamic expressions of God's will, revealed in the moment through the Holy Spirit.

For example, when Jesus spoke to the fig tree and it withered (Mark 11:12-14, 20-21), He wasn't following a formula. His words carried authority because they were a direct expression of the Father's will. Similarly, when we make prophetic decrees, we are not relying on the power of the words themselves but on the divine authority behind them.

This standpoint is what makes prophetic decrees powerful—they are not just repeated words, but declarations made from a position of authority and faith. When we decree from this standpoint, we can be assured that our words will accomplish what God intends, because they are spoken with the authority and power of the Kingdom.

This distinction is crucial because it shifts the focus from a mechanical repetition of words to a relational connection with God. A prophetic decree is an act of faith that flows naturally from our understanding of God's heart and our position in Christ.

## Prophetic Decree and Prophetic Proclamation

While a prophetic decree is a specific, authoritative command, a prophetic proclamation involves the public announcement and declaration of that decree.

In the Bible, royal decrees were often followed by proclamations that ensured the decree was communicated and enacted throughout the kingdom.

For example, when King Cyrus issued the decree to rebuild the temple, it was followed by a proclamation that mobilized the people and resources needed for the task (Ezra 1:1-4). Similarly, prophetic proclamations in the spiritual realm can amplify the power of a decree, spreading its influence and impact.

Prophetic proclamation allows God's people to respond and position themselves for the fulfillment of His purposes. It's not enough to make a decree in private prayer; often, there is power in publicly proclaiming God's will, as it activates faith and obedience within the community of believers.

Moreover, prophetic proclamation can serve as a reminder and reinforcement of what God has decreed. As we continue to declare and proclaim His Word, we align our hearts and minds with His purposes, creating an atmosphere where His will can be fully realized.

The combination of prophetic decree and proclamation is a powerful tool in the believer's arsenal. It not only establishes God's will but also spreads its influence, mobilizing others and keeping the decree active until it is fully realized.

## The Transformative Power of Speaking the Word of God Aloud

The Bible emphasizes the power of the spoken word. In Genesis 1, God spoke the world into existence with His words: *"And God said, 'Let there be light,' and there was light"* (Genesis 1:3). This act of creation through the spoken word sets a precedent for the power of decrees. When we speak God's Word aloud, we are engaging in a similar act of creation, declaring His will and bringing it into reality.

The spoken Word of God is not just a repetition of Scripture; it is a powerful declaration that has the ability to transform situations, bring healing, and manifest God's promises. Hebrews 4:12 tells us that the Word of God is *"alive and active, sharper than any double-edged sword."* When we speak God's Word, we release its inherent power to accomplish His purposes.

Decreeing the Word of God aloud is a way of partnering with God in His work on earth. It aligns our speech with His will, and through the authority given to us as believers, it sets in motion the fulfillment of His promises. The transformation that follows is a testament to the power that lies in speaking God's Word over our lives and circumstances.

## Understanding the Science Behind Spoken Words

Beyond the spiritual significance, there is a scientific basis for the power of spoken words. Research in the field of quantum physics suggests that words and thoughts carry energy that can influence the material world. This aligns with the biblical principle that life and death are in the power of the tongue (Proverbs 18:21).

Studies have shown that positive speech can have a profound impact on our mental and physical well-being. For example, words spoken with intent can influence our brain chemistry, affecting our mood, stress levels, and overall health. This is because our brain responds to the words we speak, reinforcing certain neural pathways that can either empower or weaken us.

In the spiritual realm, this scientific understanding underscores the importance of speaking life-giving words. When we decree God's Word, we are not only engaging the spiritual forces but also influencing our physical reality. The vibrations and energy released through our speech have the potential to shape our environment, attract positive outcomes, and align our lives with God's will.

Understanding the science behind spoken words provides a deeper appreciation for the practice of making decrees. It reveals that our words have real, measurable effects, both spiritually and physically, making it even more important to speak intentionally and in alignment with God's truth.

## The Reality of the Spirit World and the Power of Decrees

The reality of the spirit world is often best understood by recognizing the intangible yet powerful forces that govern much of our lives. Consider the influence of love, which binds people together through the invisible connections of family, friendship, nationality, race, and religion. These unseen forces shape our beliefs, relationships, traditions, and cultures, influencing our actions and decisions in profound ways. Just as the physical environment is shaped by internal forces, so too is the world of humanity directed by the realm of mind and spirit. The spiritual realm is, in fact, causal to the physical world.

Hebrews 11:3 (AMPC) states, *"By faith we understand that the worlds [during the successive ages] were framed (fashioned, put in order, and equipped for their intended purpose) by the word of God, so that what we see was not made out of things which are visible."* This scripture underlines the reality that the visible world is shaped by the invisible, by the spoken word of God.

Scripture is a dynamic force that creates change in both the physical and spiritual realms when spoken aloud. When you decree God's word and will, the Holy Spirit's power is unleashed to bring those decrees to fruition. Jesus Himself said, *"The words that I speak unto you, they are spirit, and they are life"* (John 6:63). This means that the substance of our words moves into the spiritual realm, creating life and manifesting God's purposes on earth.

As believers, we are created in God's image, and just as God SPOKE the world into existence, our words carry the same creative power. Whether we are conscious of it or not, every word we speak releases energy into the atmosphere, influencing the spiritual and physical worlds. Hebrews 11:3 reminds us that "*the universe was created by the word of God, so that what is seen was not made out of things that are visible.*" Our thoughts and words, though invisible, create tangible, visible realities in our lives.

## The Purpose and Power of Decrees

Now that you know what a decree is, the next question should be: What is the purpose of decrees? Decrees hold incredible power, especially when followed by proclamation—the official declaration, announcement, and speaking aloud of the decree's words. In this section, I would like to discuss this incredible power of decrees.

When I refer to the incredible power of decrees, I am talking about their purpose. Purpose is the reason for which something exists or is done. Therefore, I will be discussing the reasons why we make decrees. In other words, what do decrees do? When we make decrees, what should we expect them to accomplish? There are five key reasons why we should make decrees:

## 1. Decrees Create and Change the Spiritual and Physical Realms

Man is essentially a spirit who has a soul and lives in a body. With our body, we relate to the physical realm, and with our spirit, we relate to the spiritual realm. This means there are two types of realms: the physical and the spiritual. According to the English dictionary, the word "realm" means:

- A royal domain; kingdom.

- An area of land overseen by a king or queen.

- The region, sphere, or domain within which anything occurs, prevails, or dominates.

In light of these definitions, we have the physical royal domain or kingdom and the spiritual royal domain or kingdom. The spiritual realm controls the physical realm. The physical realm is known to man through their five senses, while the spiritual realm is known as an invisible spiritual realm, or simply the spirit world. However, the spiritual realm is not a world of fantasy or imagination but a complete and real environment for the human spirit. It is important to understand that the spirit world is a separate and real realm of existence from the physical realm, but it interfaces with the physical world.

When we make decrees, they create and make changes in both the spiritual and physical realms. How? Let me explain. First, we need to understand how these two realms came to be. God spoke the world into existence. The Bible, speaking in the book of Hebrews, says:

*"By faith we understand that the worlds were framed by the word of God, so that the things which are seen were not made of things which are visible." —Hebrews 11:3 (New King James Version, NKJV)*

Notice the "s" in the word "worlds," indicating more than one. The Bible doesn't say, "By faith we understand that the world was framed by the word of God," but rather, "By faith we understand that the worlds were framed by the word of God." The term "worlds" here refers to both the physical and spiritual realms. Also, the word "framed" in this scripture means fashioned, put in order, and equipped for their intended purpose. So, it was God's word that created the worlds. It was the spoken word of God that created the earth, its fullness, the world, and those who dwell in it.

The book of Genesis confirms this:

*"In the beginning God created the heavens and the earth. The earth was without form, and void; and darkness was on the face of the deep. And the Spirit of God was hovering over the face of the waters. Then God said, 'Let there be light'; and there was light." —Genesis 1:1-3 (NKJV)*

This passage provides the account of what happened at creation. In the beginning, the earth was without form and void, with darkness over the face of the deep.

The Bible says, *"Then God said, 'Let there be light,'"* and instantly, there was light. The rest of the world was created through this same pattern. The Bible states in verses 6, 9, 11, 14, 20, 24, and 26 of Genesis, *"Then God said..."* God spoke what He wanted into existence, and it was so. This is what Hebrews 11:3 means when it says, *"so that the things which are seen were not made of things which are visible."* Initially, these things were not visible; God called them forth, and they became visible. So, God used His word to frame the worlds—both the physical and the spiritual realms.

Decrees have a dual impact on both the spiritual and physical realms. When we decree, we are declaring God's will, which initiates a chain reaction in the spiritual realm. This can lead to the release of blessings, the binding of negative forces, and the manifestation of God's promises in the physical world.

In the spiritual realm, decrees are powerful because they carry the authority of God's Word. Ephesians 6:17 describes the Word of God as *"the sword of the Spirit,"* a weapon that we wield in spiritual warfare. When we decree God's Word, we engage in spiritual combat, cutting through the darkness and establishing God's Kingdom.

In the physical realm, decrees can bring about tangible changes. For example, decreeing healing Scriptures can lead to physical recovery, as the body responds to the spoken Word of God. Decrees can also impact circumstances, relationships, and environments, bringing them into alignment with God's will.

The connection between the spiritual and physical realms means that what we speak has the power to influence both. By making decrees, we are exercising our God-given authority to shape the world around us, bringing the realities of heaven to earth.

## 2. Decrees Express Kingdom Authority

The authority of a prophetic decree comes from the recognition of our identity as royal sons and daughters of the King of Kings. When we understand that we are seated with Christ in heavenly places (Ephesians 2:6), we begin to operate from a position of authority rather than desperation.

This Kingdom authority is not something we wield independently or for our own purposes. It is derived from our submission to Christ and is exercised in His name. Jesus Himself declared, *"All authority in heaven and on earth has been given to me"* (Matthew 28:18), and He has delegated this authority to us as His representatives on earth.

When a king speaks, his subjects must obey. Similarly, when we issue a prophetic decree in alignment with God's will, the spiritual realm must respond. Miracles, breakthroughs, and divine interventions are the natural outcomes of decrees spoken with Kingdom authority.

However, it's crucial to remember that this authority is not about commanding God to do our bidding. Instead, it's about partnering with God to declare and establish His will on earth. Our decrees are powerful because they flow from a place of intimacy with the Father and are rooted in His divine intentions.

### 3. Decrees Release and Commission Angels

Angels are ministering spirits sent to serve those who will inherit salvation (Hebrews 1:14). They respond to the Word of God and are commissioned through our decrees. Psalm 103:20 says, *"Bless the Lord, you His angels, who excel in strength, who do His word, heeding the voice of His word."*

When we speak God's Word through decrees, we activate angelic forces to carry out His commands. Angels are dispatched to execute the decrees we make in alignment with God's will, whether it's for protection, provision, or deliverance.

This understanding highlights the strategic role of decrees in spiritual warfare. As we decree God's Word, we release angelic assistance, ensuring that God's purposes are fulfilled. The commissioning of angels through our decrees is a powerful tool in the believer's arsenal, enabling us to engage the supernatural realm in the fulfillment of God's will on earth.

When we decree God's word, we do more than just speak into the atmosphere—we actively commission angels to bring those words to pass. Angels are spiritual beings created to obey God's commands, and when we speak His word, we give them something to act upon.

One of the most powerful things you can do to transform your life is to speak and decree specific scriptures into areas where you seek change. This is not just a repetitive exercise; it's a spiritual act that releases angels to fulfill God's word in your life. Angels respond not to our thoughts but to the spoken word of God. When you speak scripture aloud, you are giving angels clear instructions to carry out God's will in your situation.

## 4. Decrees Unlock Kingdom Resources

One of the most powerful aspects of prophetic decrees is their ability to unlock the resources of the Kingdom of God. These resources are not limited to material wealth but include spiritual blessings, divine favor, angelic assistance, and more. When we decree according to God's will, we open the door for these resources to be released and manifested in our lives.

The Bible offers numerous examples of how prophetic decrees have unlocked Kingdom resources. For instance, when King Hezekiah issued a decree inviting Israel and Judah to return to Jerusalem for the Passover, it resulted in a national revival (2 Chronicles 30-31). This decree mobilized the people, resources, and even the spiritual realm to bring about a significant move of God.

Similarly, in the book of Esther, Mordecai's decree, issued in the king's name, empowered the Jews to defend themselves against their enemies (Esther 8). This decree not only provided protection but also turned the plans of their enemies into victory for God's people.

Prophetic decrees, therefore, are powerful tools that believers can use to access and release the resources of heaven. Whether it's divine provision, healing, or breakthrough, these resources are made available when we decree in alignment with God's will.

So, prophetic decrees do more than declare what is; they unlock the resources of the Kingdom of Heaven. The Bible provides powerful examples of how decrees made by kings led to the fulfillment of God's purposes, accompanied by the release of heavenly resources.

In the book of Ezra, King Cyrus issued a royal decree to rebuild the temple in Jerusalem. This decree was backed by royal resources, prompting the people to give generously and volunteer for the work (Ezra 1). Similarly, King Hezekiah's decree for Israel and Judah to repent and celebrate Passover resulted in a national revival and the destruction of altars dedicated to false gods (2 Chronicles 30-31). In the book of Esther, Mordecai's decree in the king's name mobilized the Jews to overturn their enemies' plans, leading to a great victory for God's people (Esther 8).

A prophetic decree is a royal command that carries the authority of Heaven. When you make a decree based on God's Word, you are tapping into the same power that enabled these biblical leaders to bring about God's will. Your words can change atmospheres, shift situations, and break through opposition. Just as the decrees of kings in the Bible unlocked resources, brought about revival, and defeated enemies, your prophetic decrees can unlock the resources of the Kingdom, positioning you to fulfill God's purposes.

## 5. Decrees Change Your Beliefs and Reality

The words we speak not only influence the external world but also have a profound impact on our internal beliefs and reality. Repeatedly decreeing God's Word can reshape our mindset, align our thoughts with God's truth, and transform our inner world.

Romans 12:2 urges us to *"be transformed by the renewing of your mind."* One way to renew our mind is through the practice of making decrees. As we speak God's promises, we reinforce them in our minds, replacing doubt, fear, and negativity with faith, hope, and confidence in God's Word.

Over time, these decrees change our beliefs, which in turn alters our reality. When we believe God's promises, we begin to live in alignment with them, and they become manifested in our lives. This transformation process is a powerful testimony to the impact of decrees on both our inner and outer worlds.

Decrees are a form of spiritual discipline that, when practiced consistently, lead to a renewed mind and a transformed life. By speaking God's Word, we not only declare His will but also internalize it, allowing it to shape our beliefs and, ultimately, our reality.

The reality of the spirit world is deeply intertwined with the power of our words. When we speak and decree God's Word, we are not only declaring His promises but also releasing spiritual forces that bring those promises to pass. Decrees release angels to fulfill God's will, transform our beliefs to align with His truth, and unlock the resources of the Kingdom to bring about His purposes in our lives.

As you continue to speak God's Word with faith, remember that you are engaging with a spiritual reality that is far greater than what is visible. Your words carry the creative power of God Himself, and as you decree His Word, you are partnering with Heaven to see His Kingdom come and His will be done on earth as it is in Heaven.

# CHAPTER 7

# HOW KINGS PRAY

As believers who are kings in the Kingdom of God, our approach to prayer is vastly different from that of those who do not understand their royal identity. The way kings pray is rooted in a deep understanding of the authority they carry and their position in Christ. A king does not pray from a place of lack or desperation; rather, he prays from a position of dominion, authority, and victory. This mindset is crucial for effective prayer because it aligns our prayers with the truth of who we are in Christ.

In the spiritual realm, those who are in Christ are called to exercise the authority of kings. This authority is not something we strive to attain; it is a gift that has been bestowed upon us by God. When we pray, we are not merely making requests; we are issuing commands and decrees that carry the weight of divine authority. This kind of prayer is marked by confidence, boldness, and an unwavering belief in the power of God's Word.

When we understand the authority of our prayers, we begin to see them as powerful tools for bringing God's will to pass on earth. This understanding shifts our prayer life from a posture of begging to one of commanding. We recognize that our words, when spoken in faith and in alignment with God's will, have the power to change circumstances, bring about healing, and release God's blessings.

## The Language of Thanksgiving

Thanksgiving is a fundamental aspect of how kings pray. When we begin our prayers with thanksgiving, we acknowledge God's goodness and faithfulness in our lives. This sets the tone for our entire prayer, focusing our attention on God's power and provision rather than on our problems.

Kings recognize that they have already been blessed with every spiritual blessing in Christ (Ephesians 1:3). Therefore, their prayers are not filled with complaints or requests for things they believe they lack. Instead, they are filled with gratitude for what God has already done. This gratitude is not just for past blessings but also for the answers to prayers that are yet to manifest.

Beginning with thanksgiving also positions us to receive more of God's goodness. When we thank God in advance for the things we are believing Him for, we are expressing our faith in His ability and willingness to bring those things to pass. This act of faith pleases God and opens the door for Him to do even greater things in our lives.

For example, a king might begin his prayer by saying, *"Father, I thank You for the abundant life You have given me. I thank You for Your provision, Your protection, and Your peace that surpasses all understanding. I am grateful for the health, success, and prosperity that You have already provided for me. I thank You that as I speak, my words are backed by Your authority, and they shall come to pass."*

This kind of prayer is not just a reflection of a thankful heart; it is also a powerful declaration of faith that sets the stage for the rest of the prayer.

## Decrees and Declarations: The Authority of Kings

Kings do not beg; they make decrees. This principle is at the heart of royal prayers. A decree is an authoritative order issued by someone in a position of authority. In the same way, when we pray, we are issuing decrees that have the power to bring about God's will on earth.

The Bible says in Job 22:28, "*You will also decree a thing, and it will be established for you; and light will shine on your ways.*" This scripture highlights the authority we have as kings to speak things into existence. When we make decrees, we are not hoping or wishing for something to happen; we are commanding it to happen in the name of Jesus.

For example, instead of asking God to bring peace into our lives, we decree peace. We say, "*I decree peace in my home, peace in my mind, and peace in my workplace, in the name of Jesus!*" This is not a request; it is a command that must be obeyed because it is backed by the authority of heaven.

Decrees are powerful because they are based on God's Word. When we decree healing, provision, protection, or any other promise of God, we are aligning our words with His will. This alignment is what gives our decrees their power. They are not mere words; they are authoritative commands that must be obeyed.

As kings, it is our responsibility to use our words to bring about God's will on earth. We do this by making decrees that are rooted in the truth of God's Word. Whether we are decreeing healing, success, protection, or provision, we do so with the confidence that our words have the power to bring these things to pass.

In summary, the prayer of a king is characterized by thanksgiving, authority, and declarations that align with God's Word. Kings don't beg—they command. They don't react—they respond with the confidence of those who know that all of heaven back their words. As you cultivate this kingly mindset, your prayers will become more powerful, and you will see greater manifestations of God's Kingdom in your life.

## How to Pray Like a Royal Priest

Praying in the Spirit is the foundation of a royal priest's prayer life. It transcends the natural realm of worry, fear, and anxiety and elevates the believer to a place of divine authority and communion with God. The Bible instructs us in Ephesians 6:18 to *"pray always with all prayer and supplication in the Spirit."* This type of prayer is not merely about speaking in tongues; it is about aligning your prayers with the Holy Spirit's guidance, praying from a position of being seated with Christ in heavenly places (Ephesians 2:6).

When we pray in the Spirit, we are not reacting to the circumstances around us; instead, we are commanding those circumstances to align with God's will. For instance, when faced with challenges or threats, rather than praying out of fear, we should declare the truth of God's Word: *"Greater is He that is in me than he that is in the world"* (1 John 4:4). This approach to prayer reflects our understanding that we are not subject to the enemy's schemes but are victors through Christ.

## The Royal Priesthood: Praying with Authority

As royal priests, our prayers carry the authority of heaven. We do not pray from a place of begging or uncertainty but from a place of divine authority and power. This means that when we pray for others, we don't merely ask God to act; we declare His Word over the situation. For example, when praying for protection or healing, we might say, *"Father, in the name of Jesus, no evil shall befall this person; no weapon fashioned against them shall prosper"* (Isaiah 54:17). This is the language of a royal priest—confident, authoritative, and in full alignment with God's Word.

Understanding this authority is crucial because it transforms our prayers from mere petitions to powerful declarations that can change circumstances. As royal priests, we are called to intercede with the knowledge that our words are backed by the power of God. Our intercession is not just a request; it is an exercise of divine authority that commands the forces of heaven to act according to God's will.

## Interceding as a Priest, Declaring as a King

In your role as a royal priest, you are called to both intercede and declare. As a priest, you intercede on behalf of others, standing in the gap and bringing their needs before God. As a king, you declare God's will into existence, knowing that your words have the power to create and transform. This dual role is reflected in the way you pray for your community, your family, and your church. For example, when praying for your community, you might say, *"Father, I pray in the name of Jesus that Your angels will surround this place. The presence of the Lord is here, and no harm shall come near us."* This prayer combines intercession with a royal declaration, expressing both compassion and authority.

## Praying for Specific Needs with Kingly Authority

When praying for specific needs, such as the health of expectant mothers or financial breakthroughs, you should do so with both compassion and authority. For instance, in praying for an expectant mother, you might declare, *"We intercede: no complications! We decree in the name of Jesus that every pregnancy will carry to full term, and the child will be born healthy, strong, and a blessing to the family in the name of Jesus!"* This prayer reflects the dual role of the royal priest—interceding with care and declaring with authority.

The power in these prayers lies in their alignment with God's Word and the authority that has been given to you as a believer. When you pray with this understanding, you are not merely hoping for a positive outcome; you are commanding it with the confidence that it will be established according to God's will.

## Decreeing God's Will for the Church

As a royal priest, you also have the authority to decree God's will for the church and the spread of the Gospel. For example, you might pray, *"Father, in the name of Jesus, we decree that every person who heard the Gospel this week will retain the Word in their hearts. No devil will steal the Word from them! We declare that they will come to church, and they will grow in their faith, in the name of Jesus!"* This prayer is not only an intercession for those who have heard the Gospel but also a royal decree that no force of darkness will hinder their spiritual growth.

Decreeing God's will for the church is a powerful way to align with His purposes on earth. When you decree, you are not just expressing a wish; you are enforcing God's will in the spiritual realm, bringing it into manifestation in the physical world. This practice empowers you to partner with God in the expansion of His Kingdom and the fulfillment of His promises.

# CHAPTER 8

# PRACTICAL STEPS TO MAKING A PROPHETIC DECREE

A prophetic decree is a powerful spiritual declaration that carries the weight of Kingdom authority. The term 'prophetic' signifies that the decree aligns with God's will, as revealed through the Holy Spirit. When we make prophetic decrees, we are speaking out what God has shown us, bringing His intentions into manifestation on earth.

As Proverbs 18:21 tells us, *"Life and death are in the power of the tongue."* The words we speak have the power to create, to release resources, and to unlock supernatural breakthroughs.

Making a prophetic decree is a powerful act that aligns believers with the authority and will of God. It is not merely about speaking words but about declaring with the authority that comes from understanding one's position in Christ and discerning the will of the Father. This chapter provides a step-by-step guide on how to make effective prophetic decrees. By understanding and following these steps, you can effectively make prophetic decrees that transform situations and align with God's purpose.

## 1. Step into Your Royal Status

The foundation of making a prophetic decree is recognizing your identity as a child of God, a royal son or daughter of the King of Kings. Romans 8:29-30 (NLT) reminds us that God knew us in advance and chose us to be like His Son, giving us right standing and His glory. A decree is a royal command, and to make one with faith, you must understand who you are in Christ.

Even if you find it difficult at first, take a step of faith to act and speak as the royalty you are. Meditate on God's Word concerning your identity until old mindsets and doubts fall away, replaced by the truth that you are a child of God, and royalty is in your spiritual DNA.

The foundation of making a prophetic decree begins with understanding your identity as a child of God, a royal son or daughter of the King of Kings. Romans 8:29-30 reminds us that God knew His people in advance and chose them to become like His Son, giving them right standing and sharing His glory with them.

To decree effectively, you must first recognize that you have been given the status of royalty in God's Kingdom. This royal status is not dependent on your feelings or circumstances but on the truth of God's Word. You are seated with Christ in heavenly places (Ephesians 2:6), and you have been given authority to reign in life through Jesus (Romans 5:17).

Stepping into your royal status means accepting and embracing your identity in Christ. It involves meditating on scriptures that affirm your position as a co-heir with Christ and rejecting any mindset that contradicts this truth. As you grow in the understanding of who you are in Christ, your confidence in making prophetic decrees will also grow, allowing you to speak with boldness and authority.

## 2. Discern Your Father's Intention

Before making a prophetic decree, it is crucial to seek and understand the intention of the Father. Jesus taught His disciples to pray, *"Your kingdom come, Your will be done on earth as it is in heaven"* (Matthew 6:10). This prayer is a model for prophetic decrees, which should always be in alignment with God's will.

Discovering the Father's intention requires intimacy with God and sensitivity to the Holy Spirit. It involves spending time in prayer, worship, and the study of Scripture to discern what God is saying about a particular situation. The Holy Spirit reveals the will of the Father to us, guiding our prayers and decrees.

Once you have discerned God's will, you can decree with the assurance that you are declaring what has already been established in heaven. This alignment with God's intention is what gives prophetic decrees their power. Without this alignment, our words are just empty declarations, lacking the authority of heaven.

Jesus taught His disciples to pray, "*Your kingdom come, your will be done, on earth as it is in heaven*" (Matthew 6:10). To make a prophetic decree, it is crucial to first listen for what the Father is saying. This understanding comes from an intimate relationship with God and sensitivity to the Holy Spirit. Once you comprehend God's heart and mind, you can declare His intentions into being with authority in Jesus' Name.

## 3. Align Your Insight with Scripture

The Word of God is the ultimate authority, and every prophetic decree should be grounded in Scripture. Jesus demonstrated the power of aligning His words with Scripture when He responded to Satan's temptations by declaring, "*It is written*" (Matthew 4:4, 7, 10). By doing so, He wielded the authority of God's Word against the enemy.

When making a prophetic decree, it is essential to ensure that your insight and understanding are in line with Scripture. This involves finding biblical passages that support the decree you wish to make. God's Word is eternal and unchanging (Psalm 119:89), and when we decree according to Scripture, we are speaking with the full backing of divine authority.

For example, if you are making a decree for healing, you might align your decree with Isaiah 53:5, which says, *"By His stripes we are healed."* This alignment with Scripture not only strengthens your decree but also ensures that it is in accordance with God's will.

God's Word is eternal and authoritative. Psalm 119:89 (NIV) states, *"Your word, Lord, is eternal; it stands firm in the heavens."* When you align your prophetic insight with Scripture, your decree becomes even more powerful. As Jesus demonstrated in Luke 4:4, the words *"it is written"* are among the most powerful you can speak. By wrapping your insight in God's Word, you ensure that your decree is anchored in divine truth.

## 4. Understand Prophetic Decree Comes from Your Position

Prophetic decrees are not about following a formula or getting the words exactly right; they are about understanding and operating from your position in Christ. Ephesians 2:6 tells us that we are seated with

Christ in the heavenly realms, a position of authority and power.

This position means that you are not making decrees from a place of fear, lack, or defeat, but from a place of victory and authority in Christ. It's important to approach prophetic decrees with the mindset that you are partnering with God, declaring what He has already established in heaven.

Your position in Christ gives you the authority to decree God's will on earth. It is not about striving to make something happen through your own strength but about resting in the finished work of Christ and speaking from that place of victory.

Ephesians 2:6 (NIV) tells us, "*And God raised us up with Christ and seated us with him in the heavenly realms in Christ Jesus.*" Your authority to make a prophetic decree comes from your position in Christ, seated in heavenly places. It's not about getting the words right or following a specific formula; the power lies in your standing with God and speaking from that position.

Whether you use the words decree, declare, or command, the effectiveness comes from the authority vested in you by Christ. As seen in Genesis 1, the most powerful words God used to create the universe were simply *"let there be."* The authority is not in the specific words but in the authority you have in Christ.

## 5. Use Jesus' Name in Your Decrees

The name of Jesus carries all authority in heaven and on earth (Matthew 28:18). When making a prophetic decree, it is essential to do so in the name of Jesus. Jesus Himself instructed His disciples, *"Whatever you ask in My name, that I will do, that the Father may be glorified in the Son"* (John 14:13).

Using the name of Jesus in your decrees is not just a formality; it is invoking the authority of the King of Kings. When you decree in Jesus' name, you are not speaking on your own authority but on the authority of Christ Himself. This ensures that your decrees are backed by all the power of heaven.

Incorporating the name of Jesus into your decrees aligns your words with the ultimate authority and releases the power of God to bring the decree to pass.

It is through His name that we exercise the Kingdom authority given to us as believers.

Jesus said in Matthew 28:18 (NIV), *"All authority in heaven and on earth has been given to me."* We exercise Kingdom authority not in our own name but in Jesus' Name. As His co-heirs and representatives on earth, we speak with the delegated authority of Jesus. When making a prophetic decree, do so in His Name, knowing that you are releasing a 'now' word of the Father's intention.

## 6. See with the Eye of Faith

*Faith is the substance of things hoped for, the evidence of things not seen* (Hebrews 11:1). When making a prophetic decree, it is vital to see with the eye of faith, believing that what you declare is already established in the spiritual realm, even if it is not yet visible in the natural.

Faith allows you to speak with confidence, knowing that God's Word will not return void but will accomplish what it was sent to do (Isaiah 55:11). As you make your decree, envision the outcome in faith. See the healing, the provision, the breakthrough, or whatever you are decreeing as already completed.

Seeing with the eye of faith means standing firm in your declaration, regardless of what circumstances may suggest. It is the unwavering belief that God is faithful and that His Word will come to pass. This faith-filled vision is a critical component of making effective prophetic decrees.

Hebrews 11:1, 3 (NKJV) says, *"Now faith is the substance of things hoped for, the evidence of things not seen... By faith we understand that the worlds were framed by the word of God, so that the things which are seen were not made of things which are visible."* When you make a prophetic decree, envision the outcome with the eye of faith. Believe that Kingdom resources are being released, and earthly circumstances are aligning with God's will as you speak.

## 7. Make Your Declaration

After aligning your heart, mind, and words with God's will, it is time to make your prophetic decree. Speak the decree aloud, with boldness and authority, knowing that you are not merely reciting words but are releasing the power of God into the situation.

When you make your declaration, remember the words of Job 22:28: *"You will also decree a thing, and it will be established for you; and light will shine on your ways."* Your decree, spoken in faith and aligned with God's will, has the power to bring light, clarity, and breakthrough.

Make your declaration with confidence and continue to declare it regularly. Prophetic decrees are not always one-time events; they can be ongoing proclamations that reinforce God's will in your life. As you declare, expect to see the manifestation of God's promises and watch as His Kingdom is established on earth through your words.

Job 22:28 (NASB) states, *"You will also decree a thing, and it will be established for you; and light will shine on your ways."* When you have prophetic insight into a situation, you can partner with God to release His purposes. Make your Heavenly declaration in Jesus' Name and watch as breakthroughs take place.

As 2 Corinthians 1:19-20 (NIV) assures us, "*For no matter how many promises God has made, they are 'Yes' in Christ. And so through him the 'Amen' is spoken by us to the glory of God.*" When you decree in alignment with God's will, Heaven backs your words, and miraculous outcomes follow.

Making a prophetic decree is a powerful act of faith that brings God's will into the physical realm. By stepping into your royal status, discerning the Father's intention, aligning with Scripture, speaking from your heavenly position, using Jesus' Name, seeing with the eye of faith, and boldly making your declaration, you can release the authority of Heaven on earth. Remember, your words have the power to create, transform, and bring about God's Kingdom in every situation you face.

# CHAPTER 9

# DECREEING AND DECLARING IN FAITH

In the Kingdom of God, the words of a king carry extraordinary power. When a king speaks, his decrees are not merely suggestions—they are authoritative commands that must be obeyed. As believers, we are kings in God's Kingdom, and our words carry the same weight in the spiritual realm. The Bible clearly states in Job 22:28, *"Thou shalt also decree a thing, and it shall be established unto thee: and the light shall shine upon thy ways."*

This verse encapsulates the authority we possess as kings in Christ. To decree something means to make an authoritative declaration, to speak with the confidence that what you say will come to pass. When you decree according to God's Word, you are not just expressing a desire or wish; you are commanding circumstances to align with the will of God. Your words have the power to shape your reality, to bring forth what God has already promised in His Word.

It is important to recognize that this authority to decree is not based on our own merit or strength; it is rooted in our identity as children of God and in the finished work of Jesus Christ. Revelation 1:6 tells us that God *"hath made us kings and priests unto God and his Father."* This divine appointment gives us the right to speak with authority and to expect that our decrees will be established. Whether you are speaking over your health, finances, relationships, or any other area of your life, your words, when aligned with God's Word, have the power to bring about divine change.

## The Mindset of a King

To effectively decree and declare in faith, it is essential to adopt the mindset of a king. This mindset is characterized by confidence, assurance, and a deep understanding of the authority you carry. A king does not question whether his commands will be obeyed; he knows they will be. In the same way, as a believer, you must approach life with the confidence that your words will produce the desired results.

The mindset of a king is not one of doubt or fear. It is rooted in the knowledge of God's promises and the understanding that those promises are already yours. Romans 4:17 speaks of *"God, who quickeneth the dead, and calleth those things which be not as though they were."* This is the essence of a kingly mindset—speaking things into existence, calling forth what is not yet visible in the natural realm because you know it already exists in the spiritual realm.

This mindset also involves rejecting any thoughts or beliefs that are contrary to God's Word. Proverbs 23:7 says, *"For as he thinketh in his heart, so is he."* Your thoughts shape your reality, and as a king, you must guard your mind against negativity, doubt, and unbelief. Fill your mind with the Word of God, meditate on His promises, and let your thoughts be in line with the truth of who you are in Christ. When your mind is renewed by the Word, your declarations will naturally flow from a place of faith and authority.

The mindset of a king is also one of expectancy. A king expects his commands to be carried out, and as a believer, you should expect your decrees to be established. Mark 11:24 says, *"Therefore I say unto you, What things soever ye desire, when ye pray, believe that ye receive them, and ye shall have them."* Expectation is the breeding ground for miracles. When you decree in faith, expect to see the manifestation of what you have spoken. This expectation fuels your faith and brings about the results you desire.

## Walking in Kingly Authority

Understanding your authority as a king is one thing, but walking in it is another. To walk in kingly authority means to live daily with the consciousness of your position in Christ. It means taking deliberate actions that reflect your belief in the power of your words and the authority you carry.

Walking in kingly authority begins with knowing your position in Christ. Ephesians 2:6 says, *"And hath raised us up together, and made us sit together in heavenly places in Christ Jesus."* This scripture reveals that we are seated with Christ in a position of authority, far above all principalities and powers. This is not a future reality; it is a present truth. As a believer, you are already seated in a place of authority, and from this position, you are to rule and reign in life.

One of the key aspects of walking in kingly authority is the consistent use of your words to shape your world. Your words are not to be used carelessly; they are powerful tools for enforcing God's will in your life. Proverbs 18:21 says, *"Death and life are in the power of the tongue: and they that love it shall eat the fruit thereof."* Every day, you have the opportunity to speak life into your circumstances, to decree blessings, and to command situations to align with God's Word. Make it a habit to speak positive, faith-filled words, knowing that they have the power to bring about change.

Another important aspect of walking in kingly authority is resisting the works of the enemy. James 4:7 instructs us, *"Submit yourselves therefore to God. Resist the devil, and he will flee from you."* As a king, you have the authority to resist the enemy and to command him to flee. You do not have to accept sickness, lack, or any form of oppression in your life. Use your authority to bind the enemy, to cast out any demonic influence, and to declare victory in every situation.

Walking in kingly authority also involves a lifestyle of boldness and courage. Joshua 1:9 says, *"Have not I commanded thee? Be strong and of a good courage; be not afraid, neither be thou dismayed: for the LORD thy God is with thee whithersoever thou goest."* As a king, you are called to be bold in the face of challenges, to step out in faith even when the circumstances seem impossible. Boldness is the hallmark of a kingly life, and it is fueled by the knowledge that God is with you and that His power is at work within you.

Finally, walking in kingly authority requires a lifestyle of prayer and communion with God. Prayer is the channel through which you receive divine instructions and insights, and it is the platform from which you issue your decrees. Philippians 4:6-7 says, *"Be careful for nothing; but in every thing by prayer and supplication with thanksgiving let your requests be made known unto God. And the peace of God, which passeth all understanding, shall keep your hearts and minds through Christ Jesus."* As you maintain a strong prayer life, you will be continually in tune with God's will, and your decrees will be aligned with His purpose.

## Beginning with Thanksgiving and Praise

Thanksgiving is the language of kings. When you understand your identity as a king in God's Kingdom, you recognize that your prayers should not be filled with complaints or desperation, but with praise and thanksgiving. The Bible is replete with examples of how powerful thanksgiving is in the life of a believer. In Psalm 100:4, we are instructed, *"Enter into his gates with thanksgiving, and into his courts with praise: be thankful unto him, and bless his name."*

Thanksgiving sets the tone for our relationship with God. It acknowledges His greatness, His power, and His love for us. When you begin your prayers with thanksgiving, you are not only giving God the honor He deserves, but you are also setting the stage for the manifestation of His promises in your life. This is because thanksgiving is an expression of faith. It shows that you trust God's character and believe in His ability to bring His Word to pass in your life.

When you begin with praise, you shift your focus from your problems to God's greatness. It's a declaration that no matter what you are facing, you trust that God is bigger, stronger, and more than able to handle it. As a king, you don't come before God with a list of demands; you come with a heart full of gratitude, acknowledging all that He has already done. This attitude not only honors God but also opens the door for more of His blessings to flow into your life.

King David exemplified this in his prayers. Despite the challenges and battles he faced; he was known for his heart of thanksgiving. In Psalm 34:1, David declares, *"I will bless the Lord at all times: his praise shall continually be in my mouth."* This continual praise was a hallmark of David's relationship with God and a key to the victories he experienced. As you begin with praise, you align yourself with God's purposes and invite His presence into your situation.

## Acknowledging God's Provisions

Thanksgiving is not just about thanking God for what He has done; it's also about acknowledging His ongoing provisions in your life. Every good thing you have comes from God, and recognizing this truth is central to living a life of gratitude. James 1:17 says, *"Every good gift and every perfect gift is from above, and cometh down from the Father of lights, with whom is no variableness, neither shadow of turning."*

Acknowledging God's provisions means recognizing that He is your source, not just for spiritual blessings but for every aspect of your life—your health, your finances, your relationships, and your opportunities. When you acknowledge God's provisions, you are expressing your dependence on Him and your trust in His continuous care.

This acknowledgment is an important part of your kingly duties. A king recognizes the source of his wealth and power and does not take it for granted. In the same way, as a spiritual king, you must always remember that God is the source of everything good in your life. This acknowledgment leads to a deeper sense of gratitude and keeps you humble, knowing that without God, you can do nothing.

When you thank God for His provisions, you are also reinforcing your faith. You are reminding yourself of God's faithfulness and His ability to provide for you. This is especially important during times of need or uncertainty. By focusing on what God has already provided, you build your confidence in His willingness and ability to meet your future needs. Philippians 4:19 reassures us, *"But my God shall supply all your need according to his riches in glory by Christ Jesus."* Acknowledging this truth with thanksgiving strengthens your faith and positions you to receive even more from God.

## Positioning Yourself to Receive More of God's Goodness

Thanksgiving is not only an expression of gratitude for what God has done, but it also positions you to receive more of His goodness. This principle is evident throughout the Bible. When you approach God with a thankful heart, you open the door for Him to pour out even more blessings into your life.

In 1 Thessalonians 5:18, Paul instructs us, *"In every thing give thanks: for this is the will of God in Christ Jesus concerning you."* This verse reveals that thanksgiving is not just a good practice; it is God's will for us. When you live in a state of continual thanksgiving, you are living in alignment with God's will, and this alignment opens the floodgates of His blessings.

Jesus demonstrated this principle in the feeding of the five thousand. Before He multiplied the loaves and fishes, He gave thanks. John 6:11 says, *"And Jesus took the loaves; and when he had given thanks, he distributed to the disciples, and the disciples to them that were set down; and likewise of the fishes as much as they would."* It was after Jesus gave thanks that the miracle occurred, and the small amount of food became more than enough to feed the multitude. This shows us that thanksgiving precedes the miraculous.

By giving thanks, you are also acknowledging that God is already at work in your situation, even if you cannot see it yet. This act of faith positions you to receive the fullness of His goodness. When you thank God in advance, you are declaring your trust in His timing and His ways, and this trust is a magnet for His blessings.

Additionally, thanksgiving keeps your heart open and receptive to God's voice and guidance. A heart filled with gratitude is sensitive to the leading of the Holy Spirit, which allows you to move in sync with God's plans and purposes. This sensitivity is crucial for walking in the fullness of what God has for you. Psalm 50:23 says, *"Whoso offereth praise glorifieth me: and to him that ordereth his conversation aright will I shew the salvation of God."* Thanksgiving not only glorifies God but also positions you to see His salvation—His deliverance, provision, and blessing—in every area of your life.

# CHAPTER 10

# UNDERSTANDING THE ROLES OF PRAYERS, DECLARATIONS, AND DECREES

The Christian life is marked by a dynamic relationship with God, where prayer, declarations, and decrees play vital roles in shaping our spiritual journey. Understanding when to pray, declare, or decree is crucial for living out our faith effectively. In this chapter, we will explore the distinct purposes of each of these spiritual practices, drawing from biblical examples and personal experiences. By the end, you'll have a clearer understanding of how and when to employ these powerful tools in your walk with God.

## The Role of Leaders in Equipping Believers

God, in His divine wisdom, has established a framework for spiritual growth and maturity within the body of Christ. Ephesians 4:11-13 tells us that God has appointed leaders to equip His people in areas such as revelation, spiritual gifts, understanding, and identity. As followers of Jesus Christ, it is essential to recognize that prayer, decreeing, and declaring each play unique and powerful roles in our spiritual lives. Understanding when to employ each one can significantly enhance our ability to partner with God and see His will manifest in our lives and the world around us.


## Praying: Communing with God and Seeking His Intervention

Prayer is the foundation of our relationship with God. It is the means by which we communicate with Him, express our desires, and seek His intervention in our lives. Philippians 4:6 instructs us to *"be anxious for nothing, but in everything by prayer and supplication, with thanksgiving, let your requests be made known to God"* (NKJV). Prayer is the act of bringing our petitions, requests, and thanksgiving before God, trusting that He hears and responds according to His perfect will.

Prayer is not limited to believers alone. Even those who do not yet know Christ can reach out to God in prayer, as He is always ready to respond to a sincere heart. For believers, prayer is a continuous dialogue with God, fostering intimacy and a deeper understanding of His will. Whether it is a cry for help, an expression of love, or an intercession on behalf of others, prayer is a vital aspect of our spiritual walk.

Here are some examples of prayers that reflect different aspects of our relationship with God:

- "Lord, save me."

- "Lord, thank you for your unending grace."

- "Lord, please guide me through this difficult time."

- "Lord, protect my family and keep us safe."

- "Lord, may your will be done in my life."

Prayer is foundational because it aligns our hearts with God's heart. It's a time to listen, seek guidance, and intercede for others. A strong prayer life is essential for every believer, as it is the gateway to hearing God's voice and understanding His desires for our lives.

## Declaring: Announcing What God Has Already Established

A declaration is a bold announcement of what God has already established or promised. Unlike prayer, which often involves requesting something from God, declarations are proclamations of truths that we already possess in Christ. The Hebrew word for "declare," *achvah*, means "to make known" or "to set forth an accounting." When we declare something, we are making known in the natural realm what God has already decreed in the spiritual realm.

Declarations are powerful because they partner with God to bring His promises into our current reality. When we declare God's Word over our lives, we are reminding ourselves and the spiritual realm of the truths that God has spoken. For example, we can declare our righteousness, our victory in Christ, and the promises of God's protection and provision.

Here are some powerful, biblically based declarations you can make:

- "I declare that the Kingdom of God is at hand." (Matthew 4:17)

- "I declare that no weapon formed against me shall prosper." (Isaiah 54:17)

- "I declare that I am strong and courageous." (Joshua 1:9)

- "I declare that my household will be saved." (Acts 16:31)

- "I declare that the Lord is my Shepherd, and I lack nothing." (Psalm 23:1)

Declarations require a higher level of faith because they involve speaking out what may not yet be visible in the natural world. However, by declaring God's promises, we align our circumstances with His Word, bringing His divine will into our lives.

## Decreeing: Establishing New Realities with Kingdom Authority

A decree is a legal and authoritative command made by someone in a position of power. In the spiritual realm, a decree is a declaration that carries the authority of Heaven and establishes new realities in the natural world. When we decree something, we are exercising our God-given authority to bring about change according to His will.

In the Bible, decrees were made by kings, prophets, and other figures who held authority. A decree must be made within the boundaries of the authority given to the individual. For example, a king's decree affects his kingdom, and a parent's decree affects their household. Decreeing outside of one's authority is not only ineffective but can also be considered spiritual manipulation or witchcraft.

Here are some examples of decrees that reflect different aspects of our lives:

- "I decree that peace reigns in my home."

- "I decree that God's provision is released over my finances."

- "I decree healing over my body in the Name of Jesus."

- "I decree that my children will walk in God's ways and fulfill their destiny."

- "I decree that no harm shall befall my family, and we are covered by the blood of Jesus."

When decreeing, it is essential to understand that we are not creating our own desires but establishing God's will as revealed in Scripture and through the Holy Spirit. A decree is a powerful tool that, when used correctly, can bring about significant spiritual breakthroughs and manifest God's Kingdom on earth.

## When to Use Each: Pray, Declare, or Decree?

Understanding when to pray, declare, or decree is crucial for effective spiritual warfare and kingdom living. Each has its place and purpose:

- **Pray** when you are seeking God's intervention, guidance, or intimacy. Use prayer to commune with God, make requests, and intercede for others.

- **Declare** when you want to proclaim God's promises over your life or situation. Use declarations to make known what God has already established and to align your circumstances with His Word.

- **Decree** when you need to establish new realities with the authority given to you by God. Use decrees to command change in alignment with God's will and to enforce His Kingdom on earth.

In conclusion, each of these spiritual practices—praying, declaring, and decreeing—serves a unique purpose in our walk with God. By understanding and utilizing them appropriately, we can live in greater alignment with God's will, see His promises fulfilled in our lives, and manifest His Kingdom on earth. Remember, the power of these practices lies not in the words themselves but in the faith, authority, and alignment with God's Word behind them. May you grow in intimacy with God, understanding of His Word, and effectiveness in your spiritual life as you apply these principles.

# CHAPTER 11

# SCRIPTURAL FOUNDATION FOR DECREES

The power of decrees is deeply rooted in the Word of God. To decree effectively, it is essential to understand how Scripture serves as the foundation for these declarations. This chapter explores the biblical basis for using Scripture as a prophetic declaration, emphasizing the importance of speaking God's Word with authority and faith.

## The Power of the Tongue: Life and Death in What We Speak

The Bible consistently emphasizes the power of the tongue, revealing that our words have the ability to shape our reality. Proverbs 18:21 states, *"Death and life are in the power of the tongue, and those who love it will eat its fruit."* This verse highlights the profound influence that our spoken words can have, not only on our own lives but also on the lives of those around us.

James 3:3-5 compares the tongue to a small rudder that steers a large ship, illustrating how such a small part of the body can have a massive impact. Our words can build up or tear down, bless or curse, heal or wound. This power is not limited to casual conversation; it extends to the declarations we make in prayer and faith.

When we speak Scripture, we are not merely reciting words; we are releasing the very power of God into our circumstances. God's Word is alive and active (Hebrews 4:12), and when spoken in faith, it becomes a powerful weapon against the forces of darkness. The words we speak from Scripture carry divine authority because they originate from God Himself.

This understanding of the power of the tongue underscores the importance of aligning our speech with God's Word. By declaring Scripture, we align our words with God's will, allowing His power to flow through our declarations and bring about His purposes on earth.

## Turning Scripture into a Prophetic Declaration

A prophetic declaration is a statement of faith that expresses the will of God as revealed in Scripture. It is not merely a positive affirmation or wishful thinking; it is a powerful proclamation of what God has already spoken, personalized and applied to specific situations in our lives.

To turn Scripture into a prophetic declaration, follow these steps:

1. **Choose a Scripture that Speaks to Your Situation**: Begin by selecting a Bible verse that is relevant to your current circumstances or that resonates with what God has spoken to you personally. This could be a promise, a command, or a truth that you want to see manifested in your life. For example, if you are facing fear, you might choose 2 Timothy 1:7: *"For God has not*

*given us a spirit of fear, but of power and of love and of a sound mind."*

2. **Personalize the Scripture**: Once you have chosen the verse, personalize it by putting it in the first person and applying it to your specific situation. Using the example above, you could declare, "God has not given me a spirit of fear, but of power, love, and a sound mind. I walk in His power and love, and my mind is clear and focused."

3. **Use the Present Tense:** Speaking in the present tense can add power to your declaration, reinforcing the reality of God's promises in your life now. For instance, instead of saying, "I will be blessed," declare, "I am blessed."

4. **Declare with Faith and Authority**: Speak the personalized Scripture aloud, with conviction and faith. Remember, you are not simply repeating words; you are making a prophetic declaration that carries the authority of God's Word. Declare it regularly, especially when facing challenges or opposition, and trust that

God's Word will accomplish what it was sent to do (Isaiah 55:11).

5. **Meditate on the Scripture**: Beyond just speaking the declaration, meditate on the Scripture. Let it permeate your thoughts and become a part of your belief system. As you do, your faith will grow, and your words will carry even more power.

   Memorizing the verse or writing it down helps you internalize it, making it easier to declare with confidence and consistency. Speak it out regularly, especially during times of need.

By following these steps, you transform Scripture from a written text into a living, active declaration of God's will in your life. This practice not only strengthens your faith but also aligns your words with the divine authority of Scripture, enabling you to speak life, blessing, and breakthrough into your circumstances.

## Examples of Prophetic Declarations Based on Scripture

To illustrate how Scripture can be used as a prophetic declaration, here are a few examples that you can incorporate into your daily prayer life:

1. **Declaration for Strength and Courage** (Using Joshua 1:9):

    - **Scriptures:** *"Have not I commanded thee? Be strong and of a good courage; be not afraid, neither be thou dismayed: for the Lord thy God is with thee whithersoever thou goest."* - Joshua 1:9 (KJV).

    - **Declaration:** "I am strong and courageous. I do not fear, for the Lord my God is with me wherever I go. His presence gives me confidence, and I walk in His strength and victory."

2. **Declaration for Provision** (Using Philippians 4:19):

- **Scriptures:** *"But my God shall supply all your need according to his riches in glory by Christ Jesus."* - Philippians 4:19 (KJV).

- **Declaration:** "My God supplies all my needs according to His riches in glory by Christ Jesus. I lack nothing, for He is my provider, and His blessings overflow in my life."

3. **Declaration for Healing** (Using Isaiah 53:5):

   - **Scriptures:** *"But he was wounded for our transgressions, he was bruised for our iniquities: the chastisement of our peace was upon him; and with his stripes we are healed."* - Isaiah 53:5 (KJV).

   - **Declaration:** "By His stripes, I am healed. Sickness and disease have no place in my body, for Jesus bore my infirmities and carried my sorrows. I walk in divine health and wholeness."

4. **Declaration for Peace** (Using Philippians 4:6-7):

- o **Scriptures:** *"Be careful for nothing; but in every thing by prayer and supplication with thanksgiving let your requests be made known unto God. And the peace of God, which passeth all understanding, shall keep your hearts and minds through Christ Jesus."* - Philippians 4:6-7 (KJV).

- o **Declaration:** "I am anxious for nothing, but in everything, by prayer and supplication with thanksgiving, I make my requests known to God. The peace of God, which surpasses all understanding, guards my heart and mind through Christ Jesus."

5. **Declaration for Protection** (Using Psalm 91:10-11):

    - o **Scriptures:** *"There shall no evil befall thee, neither shall any plague come nigh thy dwelling. For he shall give his angels charge over thee, to keep thee in all thy ways."* - Psalm 91:10-11 (KJV).

- o **Declaration:** "No evil shall befall me, nor shall any plague come near my dwelling. For God gives His angels charge over me, to keep me in all my ways. I am safe and secure under His protection."

These examples demonstrate how specific Scriptures can be declared over different aspects of life, transforming the Word of God into a powerful, spoken force that brings about change. As you begin to declare these and other Scriptures in faith, you will experience the power of God's Word at work in your life.

# CHAPTER 12

# THE POWER OF SPOKEN BLESSINGS

Blessings, when spoken with intention and faith, carry tremendous power. Throughout the Bible, blessings are depicted as life-giving words that have the ability to shape destinies, release God's favor, and bring about divine change. This chapter explores the prophetic power of spoken blessings, examining their nature, purpose, and the profound impact they can have on our lives and the lives of others.

## The Prophetic Nature of Blessing

In Scripture, blessings are not merely kind words or expressions of goodwill; they are prophetic in nature. To bless someone is to speak well of them in alignment with God's intentions and purposes for their life. The

Greek word for blessing, "eulogeo," literally means "to speak well of." In modern contexts, we often associate this term with a eulogy—a speech that honors someone's life. However, in the biblical sense, blessings are forward-looking, speaking into the future with the authority of God's Word.

The prophetic nature of blessing is seen in how God Himself blessed humanity from the beginning. The first words spoken by God over Adam and Eve were words of blessing: "*God blessed them and said to them, 'Be fruitful and increase in number; fill the earth and subdue it'*" (Genesis 1:28). Here, God's blessing was not just a wish but a prophetic declaration that empowered them to fulfill their divine purpose.

Similarly, when we speak blessings, we are partnering with God to declare His will and release His power into the lives of others. These blessings are not based on human desires or wishes but are rooted in the revelation of God's heart and intention for the person being blessed. When spoken in faith, blessings become a vehicle through which God's purposes are established.

Blessing is a powerful, life-giving force with creative potential, as seen in Scripture. The Bible clearly emphasizes the significance of spoken blessings, illustrating how they can shape reality and bring God's intentions to fruition. From the first words God spoke over Adam and Eve (Genesis 1:27-29) to the final blessings Jesus bestowed on His disciples before His ascension (Luke 24:50-52), blessings are central to God's relationship with His people.

As believers, we are not only recipients of blessings but also conduits through which God's blessings flow to others. In Christ, we are already and always blessed (Ephesians 1:3), and Jesus, the ultimate source of all blessings, empowers us to bless others. Here are five powerful truths about blessing, along with practical tips to help you put them into practice.


## Blessing as an Impartation

Blessings carry more than just encouraging words; they carry an impartation of God's favor and power. When we speak blessings, something tangible is released into the lives of those we bless. This concept is vividly illustrated in the priestly blessing given in Numbers 6:22-27, where God instructed Aaron and his sons to bless the Israelites with these words:

*"The Lord bless you and keep you; the Lord make His face shine on you and be gracious to you; the Lord turn His face toward you and give you peace." (Numbers 6:24-26)*

God concludes this instruction by saying, *"So they will put My name on the Israelites, and I will bless them"* (Numbers 6:27). Here, the spoken blessing carried God's name and His divine presence, imparting His peace, protection, and favor upon the people.

In the New Testament, Jesus also demonstrated the power of spoken blessing. His final act before ascending to heaven was to bless His disciples: *"When He had led them out to the vicinity of Bethany, He lifted up His hands and blessed them"* (Luke 24:50). This blessing was an impartation of divine favor and empowerment for the mission ahead.

In a world where negative speech and criticism are more common, speaking words of blessing may feel unnatural. However, as children of God, we are called to align our words with His Kingdom, speaking life and declaring His purposes into existence. When you bless others according to God's will, your words carry the prophetic power to shape their future.

As believers, we have the authority to speak blessings that impart God's goodness, protection, and provision. These blessings are not merely hopes or wishes but are backed by the power of God to bring about the very things we declare.

## Blessing in Times of Opposition

The power of blessing is perhaps most evident in times of opposition. Jesus taught His followers to bless their enemies, saying, *"Bless those who curse you, pray for those who mistreat you"* (Luke 6:28). This command goes against our natural inclination to respond to opposition with defensiveness or retaliation, but it reveals a profound truth about the Kingdom of God.

Blessing in the face of opposition is a powerful act of faith that not only disarms the enemy but also releases God's power into the situation. Proverbs 18:21 reminds us, *"Death and life are in the power of the tongue, and those who love it will eat its fruit."* By choosing to speak life and blessing instead of cursing and negativity, we align ourselves with God's purposes and invite His intervention.

In 1 Peter 3:9, we are further encouraged not to repay evil with evil or insult with insult, but with blessing, *"because to this you were called so that you may inherit a blessing."* This principle shows that when we bless others, especially in times of conflict or adversity, we position ourselves to receive God's blessings in return.

Speaking blessings in opposition is an act of faith that shifts the atmosphere, bringing God's peace, favor, and victory into challenging circumstances. It reflects the heart of God, who desires to bring good even out of the most difficult situations.

## Blessing from an Abundance Mindset

A key to understanding the power of blessing is recognizing that it flows from an abundance mindset. In the Kingdom of God, blessings are not limited or scarce; they are abundant and overflowing. Jesus said, *"Freely you have received; freely give"* (Matthew 10:8).

This statement encapsulates the principle that as we have received freely from God, we are to bless others without hesitation or fear of running out.

An abundance mindset is rooted in the belief that God's resources are limitless and that He desires to bless His children extravagantly. When we bless others, we are not giving away something that we ourselves lack; rather, we are extending the overflow of what God has already given us.

This perspective is crucial because it shifts our focus from a mentality of scarcity—where we might hold back blessings for fear of losing something—to a mentality of abundance, where we generously speak blessings, knowing that God will continue to supply all our needs according to His riches in glory (Philippians 4:19).

When we bless from an abundance mindset, our words carry the power to multiply blessings in the lives of others. We become conduits of God's generosity, reflecting His nature and opening the door for even greater blessings to flow into and through our lives.

## The Role of Leaders in Blessing

Throughout Scripture, leaders are often seen as conduits of God's blessings. Fathers, priests, and kings in the Bible frequently spoke blessings over those they led, imparting God's favor and setting the course for their future.

For example, in Genesis 49, Jacob, as the patriarch of his family, spoke blessings over each of his sons, declaring their destinies and imparting God's favor upon them. Similarly, in Deuteronomy 33, Moses, as the leader of Israel, blessed the tribes before his death, speaking prophetic words that would shape their future.

In the New Testament, the role of blessing is extended to all believers, as we are all considered a "royal priesthood" (1 Peter 2:9). However, those in leadership positions—whether in the family, church, or community—have a special mandate to speak blessings over those they lead. As leaders, their words carry authority and can have a profound impact on the lives of those under their care.

Blessing is an act of spiritual leadership that brings God's will to bear in the lives of others. Whether it's a parent blessing their children, a pastor blessing their congregation, or a leader blessing their team, spoken blessings release divine favor, protection, and guidance. Leaders are called to be intentional in blessing those they lead, recognizing the power of their words to shape destinies and impart God's goodness.

Spoken blessings are a powerful way to release God's presence and purposes into the lives of others. By understanding that blessing is prophetic, carries an impartation, is powerful in opposition, flows from abundance, and is an honor of leaders, you can begin to speak and pray blessings with confidence and faith. As you align your words with God's will and speak life into the world around you, you will witness the transformative power of spoken blessings, bringing God's Kingdom into greater manifestation on earth.

# CHAPTER 13

# THE ROLE OF DECREES IN DAILY PRAYER

Prayer is a powerful means of communication with God, and when combined with decrees and declarations, it becomes an even more potent tool for aligning our lives with God's will. This chapter explores the vital role decrees play in daily prayer, the differences between decrees and declarations, and how these practices can transform our prayer life.

## The Difference Between Decrees and Declarations

Although the terms "decree" and "declaration" are often used interchangeably, they carry distinct meanings and serve different purposes in a believer's spiritual practice.

A **decree** is an authoritative statement that brings forth God's will into the natural realm. It is a command issued by someone with legal authority, similar to a royal decree made by a king. When we decree in prayer, we are exercising our God-given authority as His children to enforce His will on earth. Decrees are typically based on the Word of God and are meant to establish divine order, release blessings, or dismantle spiritual opposition.

For example, decreeing, "I decree healing in my body according to God's Word in Isaiah 53:5," is an act of declaring God's truth over your life with the authority that comes from Christ.

A **declaration**, on the other hand, is a statement that makes known what already exists or what we believe to be true. Declarations are affirmations of God's promises, truths, and blessings that we acknowledge and agree with. They do not carry the same legal weight as a decree but are powerful in affirming our faith and aligning our thoughts and words with God's Word.

For instance, declaring, "I declare that I am blessed and highly favored according to Ephesians 1:3," is an affirmation of the truth of God's blessings in your life.

Understanding the difference between decrees and declarations allows us to use them more effectively in our prayers. While both are powerful, decrees are often used to establish or enforce spiritual truths and realities, while declarations serve to affirm and confess what God has already done.

## Biblical Context of Decrees and Their Spiritual Ramifications

The concept of decrees is deeply rooted in the Bible, where we see examples of kings, prophets, and even God Himself issuing decrees that shape history and change destinies. These decrees carry spiritual ramifications that extend beyond the immediate context, influencing both the physical and spiritual realms.

One of the most profound examples of a divine decree is found in Genesis 1, where God decrees the creation of the world. Each time God spoke, "Let there be," His Words brought forth creation. This illustrates the power of decrees in bringing something into existence that did not previously exist.

In the book of Daniel, we see the decree of King Darius, who was tricked into signing a law that led to Daniel being thrown into the lion's den (Daniel 6). Despite the decree's intent, God's intervention turned the situation around, demonstrating that while human decrees have power, God's decrees are supreme and can override any earthly command.

Another significant example is in the book of Esther, where Mordecai's decree, issued in the king's name, allowed the Jews to defend themselves against their enemies (Esther 8:8-12). This decree not only protected God's people but also led to their victory, showing the power of a righteous decree in delivering and blessing God's people.

These biblical examples illustrate that decrees have the power to change the course of history, bring about divine intervention, and establish God's will on earth. When we decree according to God's Word, we are partnering with Him to release His power and purposes in our lives and the world around us.

The spiritual ramifications of decrees are significant. They can:

- **Release God's will** into a situation, bringing His plans to fruition.

- **Bind and dismantle** the works of the enemy, as we exercise our authority in Christ.

- **Activate angelic forces** to carry out God's commands.

- **Establish divine order** and bring alignment between heaven and earth.

Understanding the biblical context of decrees equips us to use them more effectively in our prayers, knowing that they carry the authority of heaven and have the power to bring about God's desired outcomes.

## The Power of Combining Decrees with Daily Prayers

When we combine decrees with our daily prayers, we elevate our prayer life to a new level of effectiveness and power. Decrees are not a substitute for prayer but a powerful complement that reinforces and establishes what we are praying for.

In daily prayer, we often bring our requests, petitions, and intercessions before God, asking for His intervention and guidance. By incorporating decrees into this process, we move from simply asking to actively participating in the manifestation of God's will.

For example, if you are praying for financial provision, you might pray, "Lord, I ask for Your provision in my finances according to Your riches in glory." To combine this with a decree, you might follow up with, "I decree that all my needs are met according to Philippians 4:19, and I declare that lack has no place in my life."

This combination of prayer and decree does two things:

1. **Prayer Invokes God's Presence and Will**: Through prayer, we invite God into our

circumstances and seek His guidance, wisdom, and intervention. Prayer is our communication with God, where we align our hearts with His and present our requests.

2. **Decrees Establish and Reinforce God's Will**: After praying, decrees serve to establish and reinforce what we have prayed for. They are a way of declaring with authority that God's will is being done and that His promises are coming to pass.

Combining decrees with prayer also strengthens our faith. As we decree God's Word, we are reminded of His promises and His faithfulness, which bolster our confidence in His ability to answer our prayers.

Moreover, decrees help us to remain focused and persistent in prayer. They serve as a daily affirmation of what we are believing God for, keeping us aligned with His Word and preventing doubt or negativity from taking root.

In summary, combining decrees with daily prayer is a powerful practice that enhances the effectiveness of our prayers, aligns us more closely with God's will, and activates the spiritual forces necessary to bring His promises to fulfillment. It is a way of taking our role as co-heirs with Christ seriously, participating actively in the establishment of God's Kingdom on earth through our words and prayers.

## Implementing Decrees in Your Life

The practice of making decrees is not just for special occasions or spiritual emergencies; it is a powerful daily discipline that can transform every aspect of your life. This section provides practical guidance on how to implement decrees in your daily life, focusing on specific areas where decrees can bring about significant change, and how to create lasting habits that ensure continuous transformation.

## Specific Areas to Focus Your Decrees

To effectively implement decrees in your life, it is important to focus on specific areas where you want to see God's power and promises manifested. Here are some key areas where daily decrees can have a profound impact:

- **Health**: Decreeing God's promises of healing and health over your body can bring about physical and emotional well-being. Scriptures like Isaiah 53:5, *"By His stripes, we are healed,"* and Psalm 103:2-3, *"Praise the Lord...who heals all your diseases,"* serve as powerful foundations for decrees related to health. Daily decrees can help you maintain divine health, recover from illness, and strengthen your body and mind.

  Example of decree for health: "I decree that my body is healed, whole, and strong in the name of Jesus. Sickness and disease have no place in me, for by His stripes, I am healed."

- **Business and Career**: If you are seeking success and favor in your business or career, decreeing God's Word over your work is crucial. Scriptures like Deuteronomy 28:12, *"The Lord will open the heavens...to bless all the work of your hands,"* and Psalm 90:17, *"May the favor of the Lord...establish* *the work of our hands,"* can be used as a basis for decrees in this area.

Example of decree for business and career: "I decree that the work of my hands is blessed and prosperous. I have favor with God and man, and doors of opportunity are open to me in the name of Jesus."

- **Finances**: Financial provision is another key area where decrees can make a significant difference. Scriptures such as Philippians 4:19, *"My God will meet all your needs according to the riches of His glory in Christ Jesus,"* and 2 Corinthians 9:8, *"And God is able to bless you abundantly,"* provide a strong foundation for financial decrees.

  Example of decree for finances: "I decree that all my financial needs are met according to God's riches in glory. I am blessed to be a blessing, and I walk in abundance in every area of my life."

- **Wisdom and Guidance**: Decreeing wisdom and guidance from God is essential for making sound decisions and navigating life's challenges. Scriptures like James 1:5, *"If any of you lacks* *wisdom, you should ask God,"* and Proverbs 3:5-6, *"Trust in the Lord with all your heart,"* can be the foundation for these decrees.

Example of decree for wisdom and guidance: "I decree that I have the wisdom of God. I hear His voice clearly, and I am led by the Holy Spirit in all my decisions. My steps are ordered by the Lord, and I walk in His perfect will."

Focusing your decrees on these specific areas ensure that every aspect of your life is aligned with God's Word and His promises. This targeted approach allows you to see tangible results as you speak God's truth into each area daily.

## Daily Decree Practices

To see lasting transformation through decrees, it is important to incorporate them into your daily routine. Here are some practical ways to make decrees a regular part of your life:

1. **Morning Decrees**: Start your day by making decrees over your life. This sets the tone for the

day and aligns your thoughts, words, and actions with God's will. Choose specific decrees that address the challenges or opportunities you anticipate in the day ahead.

Example: "I decree that today is a day of favor, blessing, and divine appointments. I am protected, guided, and empowered by the Holy Spirit in everything I do."

2. **Decrees During Prayer Time**: Integrate decrees into your regular prayer time. After presenting your requests to God, follow up with decrees that reinforce your faith and declare God's promises over those requests.

Example: After praying for a loved one's healing, decree, "I decree that [Name] is healed and whole in Jesus' name. Every cell in their body functions perfectly according to God's design."

3. **Scripture-Based Decrees**: Base your decrees on Scripture, ensuring that you are speaking God's Word and will into your life. This not only strengthens your decrees but also helps you internalize God's promises.

Example: "I decree according to Psalm 23:1 that the Lord is my shepherd; I lack nothing. He leads me beside still waters and restores my soul."

4. **Evening Decrees**: End your day with decrees that reaffirm God's protection and provision as you rest. This practice helps you to maintain a posture of faith and peace, even while you sleep.

   Example: "I decree that I dwell in the secret place of the Most High and rest in the shadow of the Almighty. No harm will overtake me, and no disaster will come near my home."

5. **Family Decrees**: If you have a family, consider making decrees together. This practice can unify your family's faith and create a powerful atmosphere of belief in your home.

   Example: "We decree that our family is blessed, protected, and walking in God's favor. We are united in love, and the joy of the Lord is our strength."

By incorporating these practices into your daily routine, decrees become a natural and powerful part of your life, consistently aligning you with God's will and enabling you to experience His promises in every area.

## Creating a Habit of Decreeing for Lasting Transformation

The key to experiencing lasting transformation through decrees is consistency. Developing a habit of decreeing God's Word daily ensures that your thoughts, words, and actions remain aligned with His truth, which in turn brings about sustained change in your life.

Here are some tips for creating a lasting habit of decreeing:

1. **Set Specific Times**: Designate specific times each day for making decrees. Whether it's in the morning, during lunch, or before bed, setting a consistent schedule helps to establish the habit.

2. **Start Small**: If you're new to decreeing, start with one or two areas of focus and gradually expand as you become more comfortable. Overloading yourself with too many decrees at

once can be overwhelming and may hinder consistency.

3. **Use a Decree Journal**: Keep a journal of your daily decrees. Writing them down helps reinforce the habit and allows you to track your progress and the results of your decrees over time.

4. **Incorporate Technology**: Use reminders on your phone or apps that can help you stay consistent with your decrees. Having a daily reminder can prompt you to speak your decrees, even on busy days.

5. **Partner with Others**: Share your decree practices with a prayer partner or small group. Encouraging each other and sharing testimonies of how God is moving through your decrees can strengthen your commitment and faith.

6. **Reflect and Adjust**: Periodically reflect on your decree practices. Are there areas where you need to be more consistent? Are there new areas that need focus? Adjust your decrees as

needed to stay aligned with what God is doing in your life.

Creating a habit of decreeing ensures that you remain connected to God's Word and His promises on a daily basis. This consistency is what leads to lasting transformation, as you continually reinforce God's truth in your life and align every area with His will.

## Examples of Daily Decrees

The power of daily decrees lies in their ability to shape our reality and align our lives with God's promises. Speaking these decrees out loud activates the spiritual principles embedded in God's Word, releasing divine power into every aspect of our lives. Below are a few foundational decrees to start incorporating into your daily routine. Incorporating daily decrees into your spiritual practice can have a profound impact on your life. Here are some examples of decrees you can speak each day:

1. **Decree for Protection**:

   - "I declare that no weapon formed against me shall prosper, and every tongue that rises against me in judgment I shall condemn. This is my heritage as a servant of the Lord, and my righteousness is from Him" (Isaiah 54:17).

   A declaration of divine protection and favor that shields you from any harm or danger.

2. **Decree for Provision**:

   - "I decree that my God shall supply all my needs according to His riches in glory by Christ Jesus. I live in abundance and lack nothing" (Philippians 4:19).

   A declaration of God's provision, reminding you that all your needs are abundantly supplied through Christ.

3. **Decree for Healing**:

   - "I declare that by the stripes of Jesus, I am healed. Sickness and disease have no place in my body, for I am redeemed from the curse of the law" (Isaiah 53:5; Galatians 3:13).

4.  **Decree for Peace**:

    - "I decree that the peace of God, which surpasses all understanding, guards my heart and mind in Christ Jesus. I am anxious for nothing, but in everything, by prayer and supplication, with thanksgiving, I make my requests known to God" (Philippians 4:6-7).

5.  **Decree for Favor**:

    - "I declare that I am surrounded by God's favor as a shield. His favor goes before me and opens doors of opportunity that no man can shut" (Psalm 5:12; Revelation 3:8).

These examples demonstrate the power of decrees in various areas of life. By making these declarations daily, you can align your life with God's promises, activate His blessings, and experience the transformative power of His Word.

# CHAPTER 14

# THE POWER OF THE NAME OF JESUS

## Understanding the Power of His Name

The Name of Jesus is the most powerful name in the universe, holding unparalleled authority and significance. When you were baptized into Christ, you were baptized into His Name, which signifies that you have become part of that Name and have the right to use it. The power of a name lies not just in the word itself but in the authority and character it represents. In the case of Jesus, His Name embodies all the authority of heaven and earth, as He has been exalted far above all principalities and powers.

The Bible tells us in Philippians 2:9-10 that God has *"highly exalted Him and given Him a name which is above every name: That at the name of Jesus every knee should bow, of things in heaven, and things in earth, and things under the earth."* This verse illustrates the universal dominion of the Name of Jesus, a name before which all creation must bow. It's not just a name; it's a declaration of authority and victory over every force, whether in heaven, on earth, or under the earth.

For believers, understanding this power means recognizing that when we invoke the Name of Jesus, we are calling upon all that He is—His authority, His power, His love, and His victory. The Name of Jesus is not just for closing prayers; it is a weapon of spiritual warfare, a tool for healing, and a declaration of our identity in Christ. As the Bible says, *"And these signs will follow those who believe: In My name they will cast out demons; they will speak with new tongues; they will take up serpents; and if they drink anything deadly, it will by no means hurt them; they will lay hands on the sick, and they will recover"* (Mark 16:17-18).

When you understand the power of His Name, you begin to live with the awareness that every time you use that Name, you are wielding the full authority of heaven. This means that whether you are praying for healing, commanding a situation to change, or simply declaring victory over your circumstances, the Name of Jesus carries the weight and power to bring it to pass.

## Why the Name of Jesus is So Powerful

The Name of Jesus is powerful because it represents the totality of who Jesus is. The power in His Name does not come from the specific letters or the pronunciation; it comes from the authority of the One who bears it—Jesus Christ. Jesus Himself declared, "*All authority has been given to Me in heaven and on earth*" (Matthew 28:18). This authority was granted to Him because of His obedience to the Father, even unto death on the cross, and through His resurrection, He has been given the highest place of honor.

Colossians 1:16-17 tells us, "*For by Him all things were created that are in heaven and that are on earth, visible and invisible, whether thrones or dominions or principalities or powers. All things were created through Him and for Him. And He is before all things, and in Him all things consist.*" This passage underscores that Jesus is not only the Creator of all things but also the sustainer of all creation. His Name, therefore, carries the authority of creation itself.

When you use the Name of Jesus, you are invoking the authority that created and sustains the universe. This is why the Name of Jesus is so powerful. It is not just a religious term; it is the embodiment of divine authority, the key to unlocking the power of God in your life. Whether you are facing sickness, financial challenges, or spiritual battles, the Name of Jesus is your guarantee of victory. At the mention of His Name, every knee must bow, and every tongue must confess that Jesus Christ is Lord, to the glory of God the Father (Philippians 2:10-11).

## The Authority of the Name of Jesus

The Name of Jesus is not just a mere label; it is the most powerful name in the universe, holding unparalleled authority both in heaven and on earth. The Bible declares in Philippians 2:9-11, *"Wherefore God also hath highly exalted him, and given him a name which is above every name: That at the name of Jesus every knee should bow, of things in heaven, and things in earth, and things under the earth."* This passage reveals that the Name of Jesus carries the full weight of authority and dominion across all realms—spiritual and physical.

When we speak of the power in the Name of Jesus, we are referring to the authority that backs that Name. This authority was given to Jesus by the Father, who exalted Him above all creation and bestowed upon Him the highest Name. As believers, we are called to use this Name in every aspect of our lives. It is through the Name of Jesus that we can command circumstances, cast out demons, heal the sick, and bring about the will of God on earth. The Name of Jesus is the embodiment of His authority, power, and victory over sin, death, and the grave.

The authority of the Name of Jesus is unparalleled and transcendent. It is the Name above every name, representing the fullness of God's power and dominion. When you invoke the Name of Jesus, you are not just speaking a word; you are releasing the very authority of heaven into your situation. This authority is derived from the fact that God the Father has exalted

Jesus, placing Him far above all principalities, powers, and dominions, and giving Him a Name that is above every name (Philippians 2:9-11).

When you speak in the Name of Jesus, you are invoking the authority of the One who is the Creator of all things. As Colossians 1:16-17 affirms, *"For by Him all things were created that are in heaven and that are on earth, visible and invisible, whether thrones or dominions or principalities or powers. All things were created through Him and for Him."* This means that everything in existence is subject to the Name of Jesus. The power behind this Name is not just in its pronunciation, but in the authority and dominion it represents.

The power in the Name of Jesus is extraordinary because it carries the full weight of divine authority. This Name is not just a religious term or a label; it is a powerful tool for believers to command circumstances, heal the sick, cast out demons, and bring about God's will on earth. When you declare the Name of Jesus over a situation, you are enforcing the victory that Jesus has already won through His death and resurrection.

The Bible is filled with examples of the apostles using the Name of Jesus to perform miracles. In Acts 3:6, Peter said to the lame man, *"In the name of Jesus Christ of Nazareth, rise up and walk,"* and the man was instantly healed. This was not just a demonstration of faith, but a revelation of the immense power contained in the Name of Jesus. The Name carries authority in all realms—heaven, earth, and even under the earth.

## Using the Name Fearlessly

To fully exercise the authority vested in the Name of Jesus, it is essential that we use it fearlessly and with full confidence. The power of the Name is not just in its utterance but in the faith and understanding behind it. When you use the Name of Jesus, you are invoking the full authority of heaven. Demons, sickness, and adverse circumstances cannot resist the power of this Name when it is used with understanding and faith.

The Bible gives us numerous examples of the early Church using the Name of Jesus with boldness and authority. For instance, in Acts 3:6, Peter said to the lame man, *"In the name of Jesus Christ of Nazareth, rise up and walk,"* and the man was instantly healed. This was not just a miraculous event but a demonstration of the power that resides in the Name of Jesus.

We are encouraged to use the Name of Jesus in every situation we face. Whether it is commanding healing in our bodies, peace in our homes, or provision in our finances, the Name of Jesus is our key to victory. Fear has no place when you understand the authority that backs the Name of Jesus. Instead of panicking or feeling overwhelmed by challenges, boldly declare the Name of Jesus over every situation and watch as the power of God is released to bring about change.

## Living in the Power of the Name

Living in the power of the Name of Jesus means that you carry the authority and presence of Christ in every aspect of your life. As a believer, you are not only called to use the Name of Jesus but to live in it. This means that every word you speak, every action you take, and every prayer you pray is done in the authority of His Name. When you truly grasp this, your approach to life changes. You begin to see yourself as a carrier of divine authority, capable of bringing about God's will in every situation.

The Name of Jesus has been named upon you, and you are now identified with that Name. Galatians 3:27 says, *"For as many of you as have been baptized into Christ have put on Christ."* This means that you have taken on His identity and are now a representative of His power and authority on earth. Living in the power of the Name of Jesus is about more than just using it in prayer; it is about embodying the life and authority of Jesus in every area of your life.

# CHAPTER 15

# JUSTIFIED TO REIGN

Sometimes, the devil may attempt to challenge your position in Christ, particularly regarding your identity as a king and a royal priest born to reign on the earth. He may try to remind you of your sins and shortcomings to undermine your confidence. This chapter is designed to affirm our legal standing of righteousness, the power of our justification, the reality of our new creation in Christ, and the empowerment of the Holy Spirit.

## The Legal Standing of Our Righteousness

When you accept Christ, you become the righteousness of God in Him. This is not merely a spiritual status but a legal standing before God.

Righteousness, as granted through Christ, is a powerful legal reality that allows you to stand before God without guilt or condemnation. This righteousness is not earned; it is a gift of grace. As Romans 5:21 states, *"That as sin hath reigned unto death, even so might grace reign through righteousness unto eternal life by Jesus Christ our Lord."*

This legal standing means that you are now in right standing with God, and this is entirely based on what Jesus has done, not on your personal merits or efforts. Your righteousness in Christ gives you the legal right to all the benefits of God's Kingdom, including the authority to reign in life. The grace of God has provided this righteousness as a free gift, and it is through this righteousness that you can confidently approach God's throne and exercise your authority in Christ.

## The Power of Accepting Righteousness

Accepting your righteousness in Christ is a powerful step in living out your identity as a king and priest unto God. Many believers struggle with guilt and condemnation, not fully embracing the righteousness that has been freely given to them. However, understanding and accepting this gift of righteousness is crucial for living a victorious Christian life.

When you accept your righteousness, you are empowered to live in the liberty of Christ, free from the chains of guilt and fear. This acceptance allows you to stand boldly in God's presence, fully aware of your rights and privileges as His child. It doesn't matter where you come from or what you've done; once you are in Christ, you are made righteous, and this righteousness grants you the freedom to live boldly and victoriously.

Remember, your own works will never make you righteous before God. Isaiah 64:6 reminds us that *"all our righteousnesses are as filthy rags."* Therefore, it is essential to rely on the righteousness that comes through faith in Christ, not on your own efforts. This righteousness allows you to reign in life, exercising your God-given authority and enjoying the fullness of His blessings.

## The Power of Justification

Justification is one of the most powerful truths in the believer's life. It is the divine act by which God declares a sinner to be righteous on the basis of faith in Jesus Christ. This justification is not something that can be earned through good works or adherence to the Law; rather, it is a gift of grace, freely given to those who believe in Jesus. Romans 4:24-25 explains, *"But for us also, to whom it shall be imputed, if we believe on him that raised up Jesus our Lord from the dead; Who was delivered for our offences, and was raised again for our justification."* This means that through Jesus' death and resurrection, we have been formally declared not guilty.

The power of justification lies in its ability to completely erase the guilt of sin and grant the believer a legal standing of righteousness before God. Acts 13:39 emphasizes this, stating, *"And by him all that believe are justified from all things, from which ye could not be justified by the law of Moses."* This declaration of righteousness allows you to stand before God as though you had never sinned. It is not a temporary status but a permanent one, secured by the finished work of Christ. This justification is what enables you to reign in life with confidence and authority, knowing that you have been made right with God.

## A New Creation in Christ

The transformative power of justification is further seen in the reality of the new creation. 2 Corinthians 5:17 declares, *"Therefore if any man be in Christ, he is a new creation: old things are passed away; behold, all things are become new."* This verse encapsulates the profound change that occurs when a person accepts Christ. The old self, with its sins and shortcomings, is completely done away with, and a new life begins—a life that is defined by the righteousness and nature of God.

As a new creation, you are no longer bound by the past. You have a new identity in Christ, one that is free from the guilt and condemnation of sin. This new identity is empowered by the resurrection life of Jesus, enabling you to live above the challenges of this world. Romans 6:4 speaks of this new life, saying, *"Therefore we are buried with him by baptism into death: that like as Christ was raised up from the dead by the glory of the Father, even so we also should walk in newness of life."* This newness of life is characterized by the ability to reign in life, as Romans 5:17 affirms, *"...they which receive abundance of grace and of the gift of righteousness shall reign in life by one, Jesus Christ."*

As a justified believer, you are not just forgiven; you are empowered to reign. You have been made a king and a priest unto God, and this new creation reality gives you the authority to live victoriously. The old limitations are gone, and you now have the nature of God within you, enabling you to walk in righteousness, peace, and joy in the Holy Ghost.

## The Empowerment of the Holy Spirit

As believers, we are not left to our own devices to fulfill the great and mighty call upon our lives. After His resurrection, Jesus instructed His disciples to *"tarry ye in the city of Jerusalem, until ye be endued with power from on high"* (Luke 24:49). This directive underscores the necessity of the Holy Spirit's empowerment for effective Christian living and ministry. The Holy Spirit is not just a comforter; He is the source of divine power, enabling us to be witnesses and proof-producers for the Kingdom of God.

The Holy Spirit's empowerment is essential for manifesting the life of God. Without Him, we are limited to human ability and natural efforts. However, with the Holy Spirit, we are infused with supernatural capability to change situations, heal the sick, and even raise the dead. This anointing transforms ordinary believers into extraordinary vessels through whom God manifests His power and glory on earth. It is through the Holy Spirit that the words and works of Jesus are continued in our lives today.

## Seize the Grace to Reign

The concept of reigning in life is deeply rooted in the abundance of grace provided through Jesus Christ. Romans 5:17 declares, *"For if by one man's offence death reigned by one; much more they which receive abundance of grace and of the gift of righteousness shall reign in life by one, Jesus Christ."* The Greek word for "receive" in this context, *lambano*, implies an active, assertive action—taking hold of or seizing something that is yours. This isn't a passive acceptance; it's an active engagement with the grace that God has lavished upon us.

Paul's exhortation to Timothy to *"be strong in the grace that is in Christ Jesus"* (2 Timothy 2:1) highlights the importance of actively appropriating this grace in our lives. As believers, we are equipped with an abundance of grace that enables us to reign—to exercise authority, influence, and control over our circumstances. This grace is not something to be experienced in the afterlife but is meant to be lived out here and now. We are called to reign on earth, functioning as kings in the Kingdom of God, with the authority to subdue every adversary and challenge that comes our way.

This overflowing grace is available to all who will take it. The key to reigning in life lies in how much grace you are willing to "lambano"—to seize and make your own. Grace is abundant and ever-present, but it only becomes effective when it is actively received. This is your appointed time to reign, your season to manifest

God's glory in every area of your life. The question is, how much of this grace have you appropriated?

The call to take this grace is a call to take full advantage of what has already been provided through Christ. Whether you need healing, divine protection, or financial empowerment, there is sufficient grace available to meet your needs and fulfill God's purpose for your life. It's not enough to know that grace is available; you must actively seize it and apply it in your life. As you do so, you will find that this grace empowers you to walk in victory, exercise your God-given authority, and reign in every aspect of your life.

## The Call to Manifest

The moment you became a Christian, you were automatically conferred with a divine responsibility: to manifest the glory of God. 1 Peter 2:9 (Amplified Bible) declares, *"But you are a chosen race, a royal priesthood, a dedicated nation; [God's] own purchased, special people, that you may set forth the wonderful deeds and display the virtues and perfections of Him Who called you out of darkness into His marvelous light."* This scripture highlights the purpose of our calling—to showcase the excellence of God in our lives.

Manifesting God's glory is not a far-fetched idea reserved for a select few; it is the calling of every believer. You are not ordinary; you have been chosen and equipped by God to display His wonders on the earth. The world is eagerly waiting for the manifestation of the sons of God, and you are that son or daughter through whom God desires to display His glory.

To fully embrace this call, you must reject any thoughts of inadequacy or inferiority. You have been endowed with everything you need to live victoriously and fulfill your divine purpose. The anointing of the Holy Spirit upon you is the power required to manifest the life and power of God wherever you are.

As a believer, you are born to manifest the glory, power, and virtues of God. This is not by your might or power, but by the Spirit of the Lord that dwells in you. Embrace this truth and let the Holy Spirit work through you to bring light to the world, transforming lives and situations as you demonstrate the reality of the divine life in Christ.

# CHAPTER 16

# LIVING AS A KING AND PRIEST

## Born to Rule on Christ's Behalf

The Bible teaches us that Christ's reign is not limited to His heavenly position but is meant to be exercised here on earth through His body—the Church. 1 Corinthians 15:25 says, *"For he must reign, till he hath put all enemies under his feet."* This reign is not just about Christ sitting on His throne in heaven; it is about Him ruling and reigning through us, His Church, here on earth.

Ephesians 1:22 further clarifies this by stating, *"And hath put all things under his feet, and gave him to be the head over all things to the church."* This passage emphasizes that Jesus, as the head, directs and governs through His body, the Church. We are the physical expression of Christ's authority on earth, and it is through us that He enforces His will and establishes His Kingdom.

Isaiah 9:6 gives us a profound insight into this truth when it says, *"For unto us a child is born, unto us a son is given: and the government shall be upon his shoulder."* Notice that the scripture does not say the government is upon His head but upon His shoulder—indicating that the authority and governance are carried out through His body, the Church. Therefore, as believers, we are called to manifest Christ's reign in our lives, exercising His authority in every sphere of influence.

When God raised Jesus from the dead, He exalted Him to the highest place of authority, setting Him far above all principalities, powers, and every name that is named (Ephesians 1:19-21). This exaltation was not just a slight elevation; it placed Jesus far above all forms of authority—spiritual and earthly. Moreover, the Bible declares that all things were placed under His feet and that He was made the head over all things for the Church, which is His body (Ephesians 1:22-23).

This truth signifies that as the Church, we are not separate from Christ's authority but are integrally connected to it. Jesus, the head, exercises His authority through the Church, His body. Therefore, if all things are under His feet, they are under our feet as well. This is not just a metaphorical concept but a spiritual reality that has practical implications for how we live our lives. We are called to live in the consciousness of this truth, knowing that we are seated with Christ in a place of authority and dominion far above all things.

## Our Position of Authority

As members of Christ's body, we hold a position of authority that transcends earthly limitations. Ephesians 1:21-22 declares that we are seated with Christ *"far above all principality and power, and might, and dominion, and every name that is named, not only in this world, but also in that which is to come."* This position is not just a future promise but a present reality. It means that we have been given authority over every spiritual force and power that operates in the world.

Understanding this position of authority is crucial for living victoriously as a believer. It means that we are not subject to the circumstances of life but are called to rule over them. Whether we consider ourselves the smallest part of the body or not, the reality is that we are still seated far above all things because we are in Christ. This truth empowers us to approach life with boldness and confidence, knowing that we have the authority to decree and declare God's will in every situation.

Isaiah 9:6 reveals a profound truth about the authority and government of Christ: *"...and the government shall be upon His shoulder."* This statement signifies that the responsibility and authority of ruling are not just upon Christ alone but extend to His body—the Church. Jesus, as the head, exercises His rulership through the Church, which is His body. If the government were said to be upon His head, it would imply that only Christ Himself carries this authority. However, by stating that the government is upon His shoulder, the scripture includes us, the Church, in the exercise of this authority.

This truth is crucial because it means that even if you were considered the least in the Church—the smallest part of His body—you are still above all things because everything has been placed under the feet of Jesus. This reality is irrevocable and unchangeable. As members of Christ's body, we share in His authority and are called to exercise dominion over all things.

Understanding your position in Christ is crucial for reigning in life. The moment you accepted Christ, you were spiritually seated with Him in heavenly places, far above all principalities, powers, and dominions. This means that you are not subject to the challenges and circumstances of this world; rather, you are positioned above them.

This position of authority is not dependent on your achievements or spiritual maturity; it is a gift given to every believer in Christ. Whether you see yourself as the smallest part of the body of Christ or the greatest, the reality remains the same—you are seated far above all things. This truth empowers you to live victoriously, knowing that nothing can overpower you because of your position in Christ.

Living in this reality requires a renewed mindset. You must see yourself as God sees you—empowered, victorious, and reigning with Christ. This understanding changes how you approach life's challenges. Instead of feeling overwhelmed, you speak to situations with the authority that comes from being seated with Christ, commanding them to align with God's will.

As believers, it is crucial to understand the authority that has been granted to us in Christ. This authority is not a mere symbolic title but a real and powerful mandate to rule and reign in life. According to Ephesians 1:21-22, we are seated with Christ in heavenly places, far above all principalities and powers. This position of authority means that we have dominion over every situation, circumstance, and demonic force that may come against us.

In this position, we are not just passive participants in the Kingdom of God but active rulers who have been given the authority to make decrees and bring about God's will on earth. This understanding transforms how we approach life, prayer, and challenges. We no longer see ourselves as victims but as victors, equipped and empowered to reign in every area of our lives.

Romans 5:17 emphasizes that those who receive the abundance of grace and the gift of righteousness shall reign in life through Jesus Christ. This scripture confirms that our authority is directly linked to the grace and righteousness we have received in Christ. Therefore, to reign as a king, we must fully embrace our identity and authority in Him.

## Reigning in Life

To reign in life means to exercise the dominion that has been given to us through Christ. Romans 5:17 says, "*...they which receive abundance of grace and of the gift of righteousness shall reign in life by one, Jesus Christ.*" The Greek word used here for "reign" is a verb that literally means "to king." This means that we are called to "king" in life—exercising authority, governing situations, and making decrees that align with God's Word.

This concept of reigning is not passive but active. It requires us to take our place of authority and to speak

God's Word with boldness. When we speak, we are not making mere statements; we are issuing decrees that have the power to change circumstances. The world and everything in it have been given to us as an inheritance, and we are called to take possession of it by faith. This involves commanding every storm, challenge, or obstacle to align with God's will in the name of Jesus.

As believers, we are not called to live passively or to be overwhelmed by the challenges of life. Instead, we are expected to arise and take up the arms of faith, being strengthened in the things of God. The Bible declares, *"The LORD will send the rod of thy strength out of Zion: rule thou in the midst of thy enemies"* (Psalm 110:2). This scripture emphasizes that we are called to rule and reign in life, exercising the dominion and authority that has been given to us in Christ.

This call to reign is not something to be taken lightly. It is a mandate from God, requiring us to speak the Word with boldness and expect to see it come to pass. We are to command every contrary storm to be still in the name of Jesus and refuse to accept sickness, poverty, or defeat. Instead, we must rule over circumstances with the authority that has been bestowed upon us as co-heirs with Christ. The world and everything in it have been given to us as an inheritance, and we are called to possess it with confidence and boldness.

## Reigning Over Life's Challenges

Reigning over life's challenges is a central aspect of living out our identity in Christ. The Bible teaches us that we are seated with Christ *"far above all principality and power, and might, and dominion, and every name that is named"* (Ephesians 1:21). This elevated position means that we have been given authority over all the forces of darkness and the challenges that come our way.

To reign in life means to exercise this authority boldly, commanding situations to align with God's will. Whether facing sickness, financial difficulties, or relational challenges, we are not to be passive or defeated. Instead, we are to speak God's Word over every situation, declaring His promises with the confidence of those who know their authority in Christ.

Romans 5:17 declares, *"For if by one man's offence death reigned by one; much more they which receive abundance of grace and of the gift of righteousness shall reign in life by one, Jesus Christ."* This scripture reminds us that we are not victims but victors, empowered by God's grace to rule and reign over all of life's circumstances.

Commanding circumstances is a key aspect of reigning in life. As believers, we have been given the authority to speak to situations and see them change. This is not a privilege reserved for a select few but a responsibility given to every believer. When Jesus spoke to the storm in Mark 4:39, He demonstrated the power of commanding circumstances. He said, *"Peace, be still!"* and the storm obeyed. This same authority has been given to us.

We are called to speak to the mountains in our lives—whether they are financial challenges, health issues, or relational conflicts—and command them to move. Mark 11:23 says, *"For verily I say unto you, That whosoever shall say unto this mountain, Be thou removed, and be thou cast into the sea; and shall not doubt in his heart, but shall believe that those things which he saith shall come to pass; he shall have whatsoever he saith."*

This authority to command circumstances is rooted in our position in Christ. As long as we are aligned with God's Word, our words carry the power to bring about the desired change. This is the essence of reigning in life—using the authority that Christ has given us to enforce God's will on earth.

## Reigning Through Your Words

As believers seated with Christ in heavenly places, our words carry the authority of the throne. The Bible tells us in Ecclesiastes 8:4, *"Where the word of a king is, there is power."* This means that as we speak, our words have the power to bring about change. We are called to reign in life by speaking words that are aligned with God's will and backed by His power.

Reigning through your words involves more than just positive confession; it is about speaking God's Word with the confidence that it will accomplish what it was sent to do. Jesus demonstrated this when He spoke to the storm, saying, *"Peace, be still,"* and the wind and waves obeyed Him. In the same way, we are to speak to the storms in our lives, commanding them to be still in the name of Jesus.

This authority to reign through your words is a key aspect of living out your position in Christ. Whatever comes against you, take charge and exercise your authority through faith-filled declarations. Speak to your situations with the confidence of a king, knowing that your words are backed by the power of God. As you do, you will see God's power manifest in your life, enabling you to walk in victory over every circumstance

## Manifesting God's Kingdom

Manifesting God's Kingdom is the natural outcome of understanding and exercising our authority in Christ. The Kingdom of God is not just a future reality but a present one that is meant to be demonstrated in our lives and through our actions. When Jesus taught His disciples to pray, *"Thy kingdom come, Thy will be done on earth as it is in heaven"* (Matthew 6:10), He was inviting them to actively participate in the manifestation of God's Kingdom on earth.

To manifest God's Kingdom means to bring the reality of heaven to earth—to demonstrate God's love, power, righteousness, and justice in our daily lives. This involves healing the sick, casting out demons, preaching the Gospel, and living a life that reflects the character and nature of God. It is about living in such a way that others can see the Kingdom of God at work in and through us.

As kings in God's Kingdom, our words and actions carry the authority to bring about change. When we speak, we must do so with the confidence that our words are backed by the power of God. This is why it is essential to speak life, declare God's promises, and make decrees that align with His will. In doing so, we manifest the Kingdom of God and fulfill our divine mandate to reign on earth.

## Walking in the Fullness of Grace

Living victoriously as a believer requires an understanding and active engagement with the grace that has been made available to us through Christ. This grace is not just a theological concept but a powerful, enabling force that empowers us to live above the limitations and challenges of this world. As 2 Timothy 2:1 exhorts, *"Be strong in the grace that is in Christ Jesus."* This strength in grace is what enables us to walk in victory, regardless of the circumstances we face.

Grace is God's ability at work in our lives, and it manifests in various ways—providing strength in weakness, wisdom in confusion, and peace in turmoil. To walk in the fullness of grace is to live in the awareness that you are divinely empowered to overcome every obstacle and to fulfill God's purpose for your life. This grace has already been lavishly provided through Christ, and it's up to us to take hold of it and apply it in our daily lives. It is by this grace that we reign in life, exercising dominion over sin, sickness, poverty, and every work of the enemy.

## Living as a King Every Day

Living victoriously also means living out your identity as a king every day. The Bible teaches that we are kings and priests unto God (Revelation 1:6), and this kingly identity is not just for special occasions; it is meant to be lived out daily. A king does not beg or live in defeat; a king reigns. This mindset should shape how you approach every aspect of life—from your thoughts and words to your actions and decisions.

As a king, you have the authority to decree and declare God's will over your life and circumstances. Ecclesiastes 8:4 says, *"Where the word of a king is, there is power."* Your words carry weight in the spiritual realm, and when you speak in alignment with God's Word, you release the power of God to bring about change. This means that every day, you should be speaking words of life, blessing, and victory over your life, family, finances, and health.

To live as a king every day is to walk in the consciousness of your royal identity, exercising the authority that has been given to you in Christ. It is to live with confidence, knowing that you are above and not beneath, that you are the head and not the tail, and that all things are under your feet in Christ. This is the victorious life that God has called you to—one where you reign in life through the abundance of grace and the gift of righteousness.

# CONCLUSION

As we conclude this journey, it is essential to reflect on the profound truths that have been uncovered. You have been called to a life of royal authority, a life that is far above the ordinary, because of who you are in Christ. This is not just a spiritual concept but a practical reality that should be evident in every aspect of your life. The authority you possess as a king and priest unto God is real and powerful, and it is meant to be exercised.

As you move forward from this journey, let the truths and principles uncovered become an integral part of your daily life. You are not just a passive participant in God's plan but a co-creator with the power to influence the spiritual and physical realms through your words and decrees. Your royal authority is not a mere concept but a reality that must be actively exercised and demonstrated.

Embracing your royal authority means fully accepting and walking in the dominion that Christ has secured for you. It means rejecting any mindset of defeat, inferiority, or powerlessness. Instead, you are to rise with boldness and confidence, knowing that you have been equipped and empowered to reign in life. The enemy will always attempt to challenge your authority, but you must stand firm in the truth of God's Word, decreeing and declaring the victory that is already yours in Christ.

Embrace the mindset of a king and priest in your daily actions. Walk boldly, knowing that your words have the power to create, transform, and establish God's will on earth. When challenges arise, remember that you are equipped with the authority to decree change, command victory, and manifest God's Kingdom in every situation. Stand firm in your identity, reject any thoughts of defeat or inferiority, and rise with the confidence that comes from knowing you are backed by Heaven's authority.

Now is the time to take your place as a king, to use your words, backed by the authority of heaven, to shape your world according to God's will. This is your destiny—to rule and reign with Christ, bringing His Kingdom to bear in every area of your life. As you do, you will see the power of God manifest in ways that will not only transform your life but will also impact those around you.

## Living Out the Reality of Your Kingship in Christ

Living out the reality of your kingship in Christ is not a one-time event; it is a daily commitment to walking in the authority, power, and identity that God has given you. This means continually renewing your mind with the Word of God, keeping yourself conscious of your position in Christ, and exercising your authority in every situation you face.

As you decree His Word, expect to see shifts in the atmosphere, breakthroughs in difficult situations, and the fulfillment of divine promises.

You have learned about the power of decrees, the significance of the Name of Jesus, and the importance of understanding your righteous standing before God. These are not just theoretical teachings; they are tools and principles that are meant to be applied every day. Whether in your personal life, your family, your career, or your ministry, the reality of your kingship in Christ should be evident.

Remember, you are not called to live a life of mediocrity or defeat. You are a king, called to reign, to manifest the Kingdom of God, and to bring His will to pass on earth as it is in heaven. As you walk in this truth, you will experience the fullness of God's blessings, and your life will be a testimony of His goodness, grace, and power.

## Your Impact on Others

Remember, your decrees do not only impact your life; they have the power to influence those around you. As you walk in your authority, you become a beacon of light, inspiring others to step into their own God-given dominion. The Kingdom of God is advanced not just through personal victories but through the collective transformation of communities and nations. Your words are tools for this greater purpose.

## Call to Action

Let this be your daily declaration: *"I am a king and a priest unto God. I walk in the authority and power of Christ. I decree and declare God's will in my life, and I see it established. I live in victory, and I manifest the Kingdom of God wherever I go."* As you make this your reality, you will truly live out the fullness of your kingship in Christ.

In conclusion, the authority you possess is a divine gift meant to be wielded with wisdom, faith, and boldness. Continue to decree and declare God's Word over your life, knowing that you are shaping your world according to His will. Your journey as a king is one of power, purpose, and endless potential. Go forth and reign in every area of your life, bringing glory to God and transforming the world around you.

# ABOUT THE AUTHOR

Nick Imoru is a dynamic speaker, author, educator, entrepreneur, and consultant based in Canada. He is the President of Achievers Centre, a division of Philips Reliability Consult Inc. Nick's mission is centered on empowering the human spirit through consulting, coaching, connecting and circulating ideas and information. His goal is to inspire, ignite passion, create profit, and make a spiritual impact, ultimately helping individuals bridge the gap between where they are and where they aspire to be.

Nick holds a B.Eng. in Mechanical and Production Engineering and an MSc. in Advanced Technology from the UK. With over 18 years of experience in the Oil and Gas industry, he specializes in Maintenance & Reliability Engineering and is a Certified Maintenance & Reliability Professional (CMRP), reflecting his commitment to excellence in his field.

As the author of over 20 books and numerous articles and research papers, Nick's work spans personal development, spirituality, academia, business, and finance. He is the founder of Achievers Consult, Achievers Centre, and Achievers Publishing, all operating under Philips Reliability Consult Inc.

Nick is happily married to Dr. Margaret and is a proud father of two daughters, Nelly and Myra. His unwavering dedication to personal and professional growth, combined with his entrepreneurial spirit, continues to make a profound impact on individuals and organizations, guiding them towards success and fulfillment.

With a vision to inspire, train, develop, and unlock potential, Nick Imoru is committed to helping individuals and businesses achieve their highest levels of success.

To contact Nick or learn more about Achievers Centre, opportunities, speeches, and seminars, please use the information below:

Email: Nick@achieverscentre.com
Website: www.achieverscentre.com

# BOOKS BY SAME AUTHOR

- A Heart for God
- Operating God's Private Lines
- Growing In Life
- Money & Pleasure: Trap of Purpose
- Success Buttons for Life & Academic Excellence
- The Making of Greatness
- Your Best Year Ever
- Nothing Just Happens
- How Did I Become Like This
- Achievers Daily Tonic
- Living in His Fullness: Unveiling the Life, Mission, Death and Triumph of Jesus
- Your Belief System: How Your Thoughts Dictate Your Life
- The Wit & Wisdom of Dr David Oyedepo
- The Tongue: How Your Words Shape Your Destiny

- He Has Said…So We May Boldly Say
- Character: The Blueprint for a Great Future
- Living in His Light: Understanding Your New Identity in Christ
- Personal & Family Budgeting: Mastering Your Money for Financial Freedom
- Your Money, Your Future: A Student's Guide to Financial Success
- Choosing the Right Path: A Career Guide for Teens and Youth
- The 21 Life Rules Every Child Should Live By
- Saving Your Future: A Practical Guide to Financial Literacy
- The Power of Your Environment: How Your Surroundings Shape Your Life
- Think It, Do It: How to Turn Thoughts into Meaningful Action
- Adventures in God's Amazing Storybook, Part 1
- Adventures in God's Amazing Storybook, Part 2

To order any of these books, please visit:

Our online shop @ www.achieverscentre.com

or any of the amazon websites:

www.amazon.ca

www.amazon.com

www.amazon.co.uk, etc